Meditations for People with ADHD

Relaxing and Confidence-Building Meditations for Those Who Have Attention Deficit Hyperactivity Disorder (2022 Guide for Beginners)

Larissa Ramsey

TABLE OF CONTENTS

INTRODUCTION

When a muscle is weak, you can strengthen it with exercises, and the same is true for the mind. Mind breathing improves your ability to pay attention. It explains how to concentrate on something. Furthermore, it teaches you to bring your thoughts back when you realise you've been distracted. It may also make you more aware of your emotions, making you less likely to act on impulse.

Meditation is known to help children with ADHD because it teaches them how to deal with and manage their emotions. If children can learn to control their emotions when they are young, the lessons will stick with them for the rest of their lives. Because ADHD is a psychological disorder, therapies such as meditation are closely linked to it. One of the most common or prominent symptoms is a lack of emotional control, which frequently leads to acting without thinking. Meditation sessions with children with ADHD may be similar to the 'think box,' in which the child must complete a task in a certain amount of time and is gently reminded when they reach the limit they have set for themselves.

According to research, mindful meditation can help alleviate the symptoms of ADHD. A UCLA researcher discovered that people with ADHD who attended a mind yoga session once a week for 2 and 2(1/2) hours and completed a regular home yoga breathing exercise that gradually increased from 1/2 to 1/4-hour over eight weeks performed better on tasks. They were also less prone to stress. Other studies that followed yielded the same results.

Yoga has been shown to improve ADHD symptoms, particularly hyperactivity, impulsivity, and inattention, and may be as effective as ADHD medication. Yoga has been shown in numerous studies to help regulate the amygdala, prefrontal cortex, thalamus, and other central parts of the brain associated with ADHD, restoring normal functioning. Yoga practised by children and teens with ADHD consistently improves their focus, cognition, mood, behaviour, and sense of well-being.

Aside from assisting people in understanding and managing their symptoms, this technique may also benefit people with ADHD:

- Improve your self-esteem.
- Reduce your stress.
- Reduce your weight.

Individuals with ADHD are critical because they have difficulty getting things done on time and may be forgetful.

However, it would be preferable if you used breathing exercises as a tool to tune out the judgmental thoughts in your head.

People who practise mindful yoga on a regular basis have been found to have lower levels of stress hormones when they are in stressful situations, such as when they feel helpless or uncontrollable.

Mindful meditation can also help you lose weight, possibly because it encourages you to think about everything you do, including what you eat.

Are you thinking about a lot of things? Consider a clear blue sky with fluffy white clouds. The sky represents your consciousness, while the clouds represent your ideas. To redirect yourself, think about the days when you had "space" in the middle of your clouds.

When you can't sit still, practising breathing exercises while walking can be just as effective as sitting. When your mind wanders, gently bring it back to the current emotions and reality.

CHAPTER 1.

THE IMPORTANCE OF MEDITATION

What Exactly Is Meditation?

Meditation is a process that allows people to calm their minds and bodies. Meditation, at its core, allows an individual's energy to be channelled towards a single focus.

To learn how to meditate, one must first understand what meditation is. Meditation does not entail living in complete silence, ignoring outside distractions, or requiring isolation or seclusion. Meditation can be practised anywhere and at any time, but beginners must first understand some fundamental aspects of the practise. There are numerous ways to meditate, but one of the most common focuses on regulating breathing patterns. This is known as breath-based meditation.

Breath-based meditation is a simple form of meditation that works by focusing the mind solely on breathing patterns. When starting out in this activity, a person will want to find a quiet place where they will not be distracted.

Eliminating as many distractions as possible allows a beginner to concentrate solely on their breathing patterns rather than being distracted by other outside influences. Once those potential distractions have been eliminated, an individual can begin to take deep breaths that are designed to immediately put their body into a state of relaxation.

Individuals must take long and slow inhales through the nose and exhales through the mouth for breath-based meditation to work.

This breathing pattern prevents people from feeling as if they are hyperventilating, which can be dangerous if it is sustained for an extended period of time. Once a person has progressed past the basic breath-based meditation stage, it will be easier for them to focus on other types of meditation.

Meditation is a natural process that occurs within everyone, but learning how to meditate effectively can be difficult even for those who have fully grasped the concept.

Fortunately, some commonalities exist among all forms of meditation that apply regardless of method or practise. One aspect of the process entails narrowing the mind's focus; this entails blocking out all external distractions and directing all of one's energy toward concentrating on one act or thought.

Another aspect of the practise that applies to all methods is that meditation necessitates the removal of mental clutter.

This includes removing thoughts and feelings that are unrelated to what is being focused on, as well as avoiding emotions or feelings that may cause someone to lose focus. When it comes to all forms of meditation, resolving internal conflicts can be a useful tool for beginners who are eager to learn how this practise can benefit them.

Individuals can progress to other types of meditation once they have mastered the fundamentals of breath-based meditation. Checking in with oneself is the best way for anyone to determine whether they are ready for further exploration into the activity.

Meditating should be simple because it is intended to be a relaxing activity that takes place in the privacy and comfort of one's own home. If it feels like work instead of an escape from stress and anxiety, beginners should keep practising until they feel comfortable enough with themselves and their surroundings to participate in more advanced forms of meditation.

Learning how to meditate, like learning anything else, can be difficult at first, but that should not deter anyone who is truly committed from completing the process.

The only way for someone to know if this is something they should pursue is to participate in a few sessions and observe what happens.

What Are the Benefits of Meditating?

Meditation has been shown to have numerous mental and physical health benefits. Individuals who learn how to meditate will notice an increase in their level of happiness as well as an increase in their energy levels throughout the day.

Furthermore, meditation can reduce and relieve feelings of depression or anxiety, making it easier for people to deal with stress on a daily basis.

Meditation also improves sleep quality. Individuals who engage in this activity on a regular basis often find that they fall asleep faster and stay in a deeper state of slumber throughout the night, rather than tossing and turning.

This not only reduces exhaustion caused by poor sleeping habits, but it also leaves people feeling well-rested and less likely to suffer from health problems such as high blood pressure or heart disease.

Anxiety and Stress Reduction

Meditation is an excellent tool for reducing anxiety and stress because it makes people feel calmer and more relaxed. This activity boosts the production of serotonin, which improves people's moods in general.

Meditation has even been shown in studies to help with pain management; aches and pains may still exist, but they become easier to ignore with regular practise.

There are numerous reasons why someone would want to learn how to meditate, not the least of which is that it is a low-impact activity with no risk of injury or negative effects on one's physical or mental health.

So, why haven't you begun yet?

Meditation is a relaxing activity that anyone can do. There are no rules dictating how it should be done, what clothes one should wear to participate, or where one should go to find the ideal location for practising this method of relaxation and focus. Individuals who learn to meditate will not only notice a difference in their physical bodies, but they will also notice an improvement in their day-to-day lives.

Meditation takes place in the privacy of one's own home, so there is nothing to prevent anyone from giving it a try and seeing what happens when they finally make time for this activity on a regular basis.

Meditation is an excellent tool for people who want to relax and learn how to better focus their minds. Let's get this party started!

Physical Health Advantages

Sleep

- Sleep is one of the top five factors influencing physical and mental health. Sleep deprivation affects a large number of people. Problems such as when they feel their body is tired and their body requires a night of deep sleep in order to be refreshed or healthy again.

- Many people develop the habit of thinking about their office work or official conversations right before bed, which causes stress, delays sleep, or causes shallow sleep.
- Many people, even if they have been in bed for hours, are unable to fall asleep quickly.
- People, on the other hand, feel drowsy while working.
- This is simply the result of people who do not get enough good, deep sleep at night.

The majority of the above symptoms are caused by work stress, distraction, and emotional roller coaster, as well as irregular sleeping habits.

Meditation creates a barrier between your daily stress and emotional roller coaster; as a result, you are unaffected by all of the factors that contribute to these sleep disorder symptoms. Throughout the day, my mind is calm and peaceful. During meditation, you will become aware of the fact that thoughts, stress, and emotions come and go in your mind. They should become attached to you. One should examine them objectively and make a positive decision in life. In this manner, one's inner self is always at ease, and sleep comes faster and deeper for him/her.

To reap the most benefits, meditate for 5 to 15 minutes before going to bed.

Energy and Weight

A person's weight and energy levels should be optimal in order to live a healthy life.

Recognize that your body is merely a tool provided by God to help you complete your worldly tasks. If these tools are not in perfect working order, it has an impact on your life and productivity. Obesity and a lack of energy are two of the most common health issues that people face today. These issues can have an indirect impact on one's relationship, social life, and financial life.

Obesity and fatigue are typically caused by a lack of knowledge about certain eating habits, such as food addictions such as sugar, alcohol, and so on. Here's why meditation is beneficial: it allows you to focus on yourself. One begins to gain a better understanding of one's own body.

One becomes more aware of what is and is not important to one's body.

You naturally begin to believe that vegetables and fruits are better for your body than fast foods/junk food. You may begin to believe that alcohol, cigarette smoking, and sugar addiction only make you feel good for a short period of time before sending you into a depression or craving state.

Sooner or later, one begins to automatically abandon these bad habits because this feeling comes from within, not from without (from friends, family, etc.), and one begins to focus on good habits that are beneficial to one's body.

Obesity and low energy levels are primarily caused by poor eating habits. As a result, meditation addresses the root cause of these habits and aids in their abolition. One can find various ways to lose weight and gain energy, such as a strict diet, rigorous exercise, pills, and so on, but all of these methods are temporary, and the effect will only last as long as you do these things (until you exercise until you take pills).

Meditation, on the other hand, addresses the root cause of these habits, and they naturally leave the person rather than the person leaving the habits.

Other Health Advantages

- Enhances the immune system.
- Reduce ageing.
- Control your breathing and heart rate.
- Lowers blood pressure.
- Longevity is increased.
- Increases energy and reduces fatigue.
- Reduces the negative impact of chronic body pain on the physical body as well as the emotional state.
- Muscle tension, stress, and headaches are reduced.
- Aids in the treatment of arthritis, an inflammatory disorder, and asthma.
- Mental Advantages

Life's Positivity

The mind will become calmer and more peaceful as you practise meditation on a regular basis. Concentration improves as a result of meditation. Focusing on negative thoughts, such as "I am not capable of doing it," "I am poor," and so on, will result in more of the same in your life. If one thinks positively, "Why can't I do this?" "Why can't I become wealthy in my lifetime?" "I'm willing to do whatever it takes to become wealthy and fulfilled," and those things will come to pass in life.

With meditation, you gain a better understanding of things as they are and a greater focus on the positive.

It relieves stress and anxiety.

13

The act of recognising that your thoughts come and go through your mind significantly reduces our stress and anxiety. You are not your thoughts, but they are a part of you.

Spending time alone with yourself during meditation assists in remaining unaffected by the outside world and in loving yourself. Meditation can assist you in bringing your problems to the surface so that you can make a better decision to resolve them rather than stressing about them.

"Answers come in still mind," according to a Buddhist proverb.

- Meditation helps to calm your mind, allowing you to hear your soul more clearly.
- Emotional Balance and Harmony with Nature
- Meditation removes unnecessary negatives thought from one's mind.

Nourishes it with positive thoughts. It calms the mind by making us neutral so that we are not depressed in unfavourable conditions or do not get overexcited or overwhelmed in favourable conditions. So, it helps to keep a balance emotionally.

Meditation helps us to understand that we are just a part of this whole universe and we cannot live without making harmony with nature. If we live unharmoniously, it will only affect our self negatively, not the nature or universe.

Meditation also helps us to accept the circumstances and things as they are. Stress, anger, anxiety, sorrow comes when you don't see things as they are, you expect those things you want to be. If you start understanding and accepting things as they are, you will be free from sorrow, stress, anger, and anxiety. Meditation helps in achieving this.

14

Other mental benefits of meditation are:

- It improves memory.
- It resolves phobia's and fears
- It controls anger.
- It develops intuition.
- It increases concentration.
- It helps to quit addictions.
- Decrease in potential mental illness.
- Prevent and potentially cure depression.
- Decreases restless thinking and worrying.
- It improves relationships.
- It improves productivity.

It helps to focus more on the important things in life instead of wasting the time of our life.

Spiritual Benefits

As you might now be able to understand that meditation calms your mind from unnecessary thinking and it helps one to become closure to one's soul, thus increase your spiritual world. It helps to be in more harmony with nature and existence. It helps to understand that there is a big power behind all existence, God.

When one spends time with oneself during meditation, it helps in self-actualization. One starts to understand oneself. Meditation helps increase in growing wisdom. One starts understanding life in much better and clear ways. It helps in increasing happiness, compassion, and forgiveness increases a sense of "oneness," decreases ego, and helps in discovering purpose in life. All these make one free from materialistic bondage and make him/her truly free.

15

CHAPTER 2.

MEDITATION TO PEOPLE WITH ADHD AND ITS IMPORTANCE

If you are a typical child or adult, you already have a long list of demands, but if you are a child or adult with ADHD, you are probably aware that you will have to work twice as hard to meet those same demands. You will most likely experience frustration, exhaustion, and stress at times, but don't give up. There are some excellent resources available to assist you on your journey.

Children and adults with ADHD are concerned about their ability to focus their attention for long enough to calm their minds and bodies.

There are some short exercises that, with practise, one's ability to process them will become easier and easier. Remember to take small steps and gradually increase your time as you become more comfortable with your new skills.

ADHD is an abbreviation for attention deficit hyperactivity disorder. ADHD is the most common medical disorder affecting children and teenagers today, according to the American Psychiatric Association (2020). If you can't focus, can't seem to stay still, or act rashly without thinking things through, you may have ADHD.

According to the APA (2020), ADHD affects more than 8% of children and 2% of adults, and it is more common in males than females.

ADHD is classified into three types based on symptoms observed for at least six months. The following symptoms are frequently observed.

Inattentive Personality

- It makes careless errors or fails to pay close attention to detail.
- It is unable to concentrate on tasks or activities.
- When spoken to, they are unable to listen and their attention is diverted.

- When given instructions, it does not carry them out. They may start a task but lose focus and fail to complete it.
- It has difficulty organising tasks/work and thus misses deadlines, is unable to manage time effectively, and may have an unorganised work ethic.
- It avoids tasks that require mental acuity or the completion of forms.
- It frequently misplaces items that are necessary for daily living, such as books, keys, cell phones, or eyeglasses.
- It quickly becomes distracting.
- It is oblivious to daily responsibilities.
- Type of Hyperactive Impulse
- It is unable to sit still and fidgets with its hands or feet.
- It will be unable to remain seated in restaurants, classrooms, and other public places.
- When the situation calls for it, it will run around or climb.
- It appears to be inexhaustible and always on the move.
- Talk all the time.
- It will not wait for a question to be finished before responding.
- It demonstrates an inability to wait their turn in a conversation or while in line for something.
- It has the potential to intervene and take over what others are doing.

Type Combination

The combined type will exhibit symptoms from both types of ADHD. Do you have a teen who has ADHD? It's difficult enough to maintain upgrades, prepare for adulthood, and attend college, but what if you have an additional challenge?

Teens with ADHD frequently have to work twice as hard to maintain their focus in school. Though some symptoms vary from person to person, many suffer from a lack of focus and concentration, forgetfulness, poor decision-making, hyperactivity, and heightened emotions. Teens with ADHD may feel like adrenaline junkies, with a slew of ideas swirling around in their heads like a Category 5 tornado. They may seek stress and drama. The thought of meditating may cause them to scream into a pillow.

However, the good news is that meditation can help to stabilise ADHD symptoms. The bad news is that convincing a teen with ADHD to try meditation can be difficult.

Don't worry, we have a few pointers to make this a more user-friendly experience. Meditation does not require you to sit in the lotus position; in fact, you do not need to sit at all! It is not necessary to have a mantra or to practise yoga. Meditation is extremely difficult—if not impossible—to fail at because it can be easily adapted to fit any personality.

If your mind is racing, try these steps:

- "Meditation is achieved through practise," repeat as many times as necessary, even if it's a million times. I intend to take what I've learned from this experience and apply it to my future endeavours. There are no incorrect methods of meditation."
- Make yourself at ease. There is no such thing as over-comfort. If you fall asleep, you probably need it!
- Find your zone of comfort. It is critical to be at ease while meditating. You'll be the best judge of what works for you. Whether it's lying in your bed, slowly walking up and down the hall, or sitting on a swing from a large oak tree in the backyard, just do it.

19

- Breathe slowly and evenly. Relax and allow your breath to flow naturally.
- It will be difficult to train your brain to quickly switch gears and settle into meditation mode. Consider creating a premeditation ritual that includes taking a hot bath or shower, putting on comfortable clothing, and listening to soothing music before you meditate. This will reduce the impact of changing states and ensure a smooth transition for both mind and body into meditation.
- Cues from the senses. Certain sensory cues may assist you in transitioning from one mental state to another. Maybe you have a very soft, comfortable shirt that you can now use as your meditation shirt. You may enjoy the sound of a light rain falling in a tropical rainforest, or you may enjoy using a diffuser with lavender. This is your meditation time, so do whatever works best for you. Instrumental music is typically preferred. Skip the lyrics because they can be distracting and undermine your intent.
- Choose your focal point. A guided recording could be your focus.
- Some people can simply concentrate on their breathing, while others can mentally repeat a word or phrase (mantra). If it's the holiday season, you might like to sit quietly by the Christmas tree and look at the ornaments and lights.
- Moving meditation is just as effective as sitting meditation. When meditating, don't try to impose what you consider a "should."
- Meditation can sometimes be most effective for the active ADHD teen through a simple, quiet, distraction-free walk.
- Maintain your focus. Especially when you first start down the path of meditation, you will most likely have to bring your mind back to focus frequently. Don't be disheartened.

Meditation, as you are now aware, becomes easier and easier with repetition.

- Initially, keep your sessions brief. For your first meditation experience, it is unreasonable to meditate for twenty minutes. As you become more comfortable with your meditation routine, feel free to lengthen your sessions as they become more relaxing and comforting. When this happens, you are reaping some of the benefits of meditation.
- Maintain a routine. If you have ADHD or have difficulty sticking to a routine, setting an alarm for the same time each day to remind you to breathe can be as simple as setting an alarm for the same time each day. If you are really struggling, there are ADHD coaches who can help you stay on track.
- Transcendental Meditation can help you change your brain. Some recent studies suggest that Transcendental Meditation can help with some of the symptoms of ADHD. According to TM® for Women (2013), there have been studies that show a link between Transcendental Meditation and brain changes.
- Brainwave patterns, particularly the ratio of beta to theta waves, have been linked to the severity of ADHD. The practise of TM appears to postpone the development of certain frontal brain changes that alleviate ADHD symptoms.

There are currently no known specific causes of ADHD. So far, there is no evidence that it is due to genetic or random stresses during pregnancy. At this time, doctors and researchers are unsure of the causes of ADHD development. What others need to understand is that ADHD is not a lazy disorder; it is a developmental

21

disorder of the brain. If you suspect you have ADHD, consult with a medical professional to determine what is going on in your life.

If you have ADHD, you can greatly benefit from eating healthy foods, getting adequate rest and sleep, staying active with some form of exercise, and practising mindfulness and breathing exercises.

If a person has ADHD, they may have difficulty focusing long enough to complete their schoolwork. The issue is that ADHD teens crave a lot of stimulation and excitement, so writing a paper on the fall of the Roman Empire can take a long time for them to complete.

Parents and teachers may be unaware that ADHD students do not benefit from the punishment/reward system in the same way that other students do.

What is it like for adolescent ADHD? When you have ADHD symptoms, you may feel overwhelmed, chaotic, and out of control. It's not that you don't want to write that paper; it's just that the enormity of the task can make you want to run around the house, dispensing a case of silly string along the way. You may frequently feel bad about yourself because you are chastised for things you cannot control, such as not listening, losing your temper, or completing tasks too quickly and making mistakes. Just remember that ADHD and its symptoms are not your fault and that you have nothing to be ashamed of.

There are some common misconceptions about ADHD. The first is that adolescents are hyperactive. Parents may be unaware that by the time their child reaches adolescence, hyperactivity has usually been replaced by restlessness. Second, it is widely assumed that teens with ADHD are unable to sit still for ten minutes. Despite popular belief, teenage students can and do sit still in class. They may, however, daydream or fall asleep. Myth three is that ADHD goes away in teenagers and adults. Originally, it was thought that people outgrew ADHD as their hyperactivity decreased.

There is currently no scientific evidence that ADHD can be outgrown, but meditation can engage an ADHD sufferer's brain.

Mindfulness meditation appears to hold the most promise for reducing ADHD symptoms. Over more traditional methods, guided meditation apps and videos can be more effective for a brain that needs engagement. People generally believe that ADHD is overdiagnosed. Because more research has been conducted, the diagnosis has only recently caught up, as ADHD had been seriously underdiagnosed for many years.

While ADHD makes it difficult to ignore annoying distractions that lead you astray, it can also cause you to concentrate so intensely that you can work on a project for hours without realising how much time has passed. This mode is known as hyper-focus. The only disadvantage of hyper-focus is that it can cause tunnel vision, which can interfere with the rest of your life. For example, you may want to look up a single fact about the Roman Empire on the internet, but before you know it, several hours have passed and you have wasted hours online, which may cause you to be late for your pre-sleep wind-down, miss your date with the cute girl in chemistry class, or be late for your after-school job. Relationships, schoolwork, and your health may suffer as a result. However, if you can master your hyper-focus, it could become your most valuable asset.

How does one meditate when they have ADHD? People with ADHD's brains can make them feel like adrenaline junkies, looking for stress and drama because they thrive on it. Teens with ADHD do not have to sit down to meditate, stop moving, or develop a mantra if doing so makes them feel uncomfortable. What you must remember is to use meditation to counteract all of the bad habits you developed while your ADHD was in control.

It takes time to meditate. Avoid overburdening your brain by forcing lengthy sessions, which can be a turn-off. Begin with a time of two minutes and gradually increase as you feel comfortable.

Set your meditation for first thing in the morning if your schedule allows.

Meditation has no set rules, so you can do whatever works best for you. If being inside makes you uneasy, take your meditation outside.

Maintain your cool and give meditation a chance to work for you. Even if you don't realise it, everyone requires some downtime.

Unfortunately, you cannot turn your ADHD characteristics on and off like a light switch, but you can become more aware of what causes you to focus on certain things. For example, you are more likely to lose yourself in activities that you find interesting, whereas others you simply mentally avoid.

Keep a list of things that catch your attention, as well as a list of things that turn you off. Can you spend an entire day doing a puzzle but only look at geometry for a few seconds before going off in another direction?

We know that being hyper-focused can cause you to lose time, so avoid engaging in triggers before bedtime or before set times that you need to be at school, work, or out with friends to avoid missing out on needed sleep.

If you suspect that you have become engrossed in your hyper-focus, you must redirect your attention, even if it is difficult.

So, if Spot is waiting at the front door, take him for a walk, do some deep breathing exercises, or empty/load the dishwasher. A change of venue will be beneficial.

Determine how much time you want to devote to a task. Assume you get home from school and want to work on your paper on the fall of the Roman Empire. However, because you become engrossed in the internet, you only want to devote two hours each night this week, right after you get home from classes. Set an alarm on your phone to notify you when you need to step away from this project due to other obligations. It usually takes a few extra minutes for the brain to switch gears, so leave a fifteen-minute gap between tasks.

Cutting out distractions ahead of time will allow you to make the most of your time. Make a list of everything you'll need for your project, and gather it all together before you start so you don't have to stop and look for a missing piece. Also, limit your digital distractions during this time. To avoid temptations, turn off your phone notifications and keep your phone out of reach.

While you may not always be able to control the things that pull you away from your goal, you can help yourself by including a step-by-step process of the steps you must take to achieve your goal. You could include some regular timeouts to help you break the spell of hyper-focus. Get up every 45 minutes or so and do something else for a few minutes. The timeout itself is unimportant, as long as it is not another task on which you typically focus intensely.

You can manage it by breaking the project down into smaller pieces, which will keep you from going over the edge. You can use this simple method to prioritise tasks, keep instructions and information at your fingertips, and complete your task.

Is it possible to have ADHD and not appear hyperactive?

Absolutely. The inattentive type (described above) has difficulty paying attention and is prone to making careless mistakes, misplacing items, and failing to follow through.

Is There Anything Positive to Be Said About ADHD?

According to Smitha Bhandari, MD (2019), students with ADHD performed better on tests, had higher levels of creativity, and were skilled in drama, music, visual arts, and scientific discoveries. According to a German study, being impulsive gave ADHD subjects the ability to hyperfocus, and their impulsive tendencies made them great entrepreneurs.

Some famous people who suffer from ADHD include U.S. Olympic champion Simone Biles, Olympic champion Michael Phelps, Justin Timberlake, Super Bowl champion Terry Bradshaw, and even Paris Hilton. They've all gone on to have astonishingly successful careers. As a result, nothing stands in your way of achieving your own personal success.

Case Study and Exercise

Case Study—Kevin

I struggled a lot in junior high and high school. My parent-teacher conferences were always heated, and I was always labelled as a slacker. My teachers didn't understand me, and they made no effort to figure out why I couldn't pay attention in class and occasionally fell asleep. I was accused of failing to pay attention in class or failing to recognise that I had been called upon to answer a question in front of the entire class.

I admit that I probably appeared lazy, but I was easily distracted and frequently irritated as a result. It wasn't that I didn't want to write my papers. I'd come home with the best of intentions, but after a few minutes of researching things on the internet, I'd become distracted, and before I knew it, it was bedtime. My college years were characterised by unfinished projects and incomplete grades. I was in danger of being held back a year, which I didn't want, so I became more depressed.

Because my parents didn't understand, I was hounded at home with negative reinforcement. What's the point? I couldn't figure it out.

My regular teacher was absent one day, so we had a substitute. She noticed my inability to focus and pay attention to detail and immediately recognised that I had ADHD. Miss Kinzie attended my next parent-teacher conference and spoke with both my parents and my regular teacher.

She made some recommendations about activities that I could do to help build my skills after explaining all of the signs that they had missed and that I was not, in fact, lazy. Miss Kinzie suggested that I try some mindfulness meditation techniques, as well as some yoga movements, to rewire the way I thought.

I was prepared because I didn't want to be held back a year. That day, something else changed in me as well. Miss Kinzie, a teacher but an unknown, had believed in me when no one else had. She had an incredible influence on my life. I felt like I was going insane the whole time. Someone had come to my aid just as I was about to give up.

27

Giving me the benefit of the doubt, I was promoted to the next grade level, allowing me to spend the entire summer working with a yoga instructor who had experience working with ADHD teens. I worked very hard before returning to school, and I felt more confident and had tools to help me deal with my distractions. There were no more unfinished assignments, and there was no more punishment. I was finally understood. As I near the end of my senior year of high school, I already have a professional goal in mind and have been accepted to three of my top choice colleges. I'm feeling revitalised and confident. It was all thanks to one teacher who noticed that I wasn't so sluggish after all. Miss Kinzie, I'm sure, has gone on to help many other students like me.

Exercise

What can I do to study more effectively at home? Break out the paper and pencils, and let's figure out what works best for you when studying at home. Make a list of everything that applies to you.

When do you think is the best time for you to study?

- When I get home from school for the first time.
- After school, but I need to take a quick break before I begin.
- Begin immediately after dinner.
- Before I leave for school in the morning?

Who is the best person for me to study with?

- Alone.
- When there is another person in the room.
- A good friend.
- A guardian.

- A teacher.

Where do I believe I will be able to study the most effectively?

- I was in my bedroom.
- There is no specific room, just on the floor.
- I'm in my bed.
- I'm at my desk.
- At the dinner table.
- In the family room, in a chair.

Is there anything else I should do while I study?

Is it necessary for me to sit?

Do I study better when I lie down?

Is it necessary for it to be extremely quiet?

Do I require a desk lamp?

Is it possible for me to work well with some soft music playing in the background?

What is the best time for me to study before I need to take a break?

- It takes fifteen minutes.
- It takes thirty minutes.
- One hour.

What can I do to stay organised and complete my homework?

- I use a planner to keep track of my assignments and deadlines.
- For the assignments, contact a friend.
- Keep extra copies of books on hand at all times.
- Plan out what I'm going to do first.
- Determine how much time each step of the assignment will take.
- Put all of my completed work in one place.
- Color codebook covers and folders are available.

What resources are available to assist me in learning/remembering information?

- Make a list of everything.
- Make a drawing to help me remember.
- Make use of flash cards.
- Enter data into my computer.
- Listen to a recording I made of the necessary information.
- Read it aloud.
- If you come up with different ideas, make a note of what works for you.

Meditation

So, what exactly is mindfulness, and how will it benefit you? Mindfulness can occur naturally, but it requires paying attention to something and observing what you are doing without distractions. Assume you are riding your horse on a jumping course. Your course has a pattern that you must follow, but you must also ride each fence individually and may have to make last-minute adjustments to your approach. The ability to tune out everything else and focus solely on the task at hand is the pinnacle of mindfulness.

When you have a weak muscle, you need to strengthen it, and mindfulness is the exercise you do to strengthen your brain's muscles.

If you're worried that mindfulness is just religious nonsense, rest assured that it isn't. Despite the fact that the roots of meditation and mindfulness can be traced back to religion, it essentially entails paying close attention to your feelings, thoughts, and bodily sensations. In other words, it refers to what is happening to you right now. Mindfulness can help you with a variety of wellness techniques.

You may be wondering why you need mindfulness, but there are some skills you will need to help you achieve.

- It improves your ability to pay attention and listen to others.
- It enables you to learn more.
- You get better at being less distracted.
- It assists you in gaining self-control and avoiding becoming easily agitated.
- It makes you happier, which allows you to enjoy things more.
- It enables you to be more patient.
- It trains you to slow down rather than always rushing.
- When confronted with a stressful situation, you maintain your cool.
- You stop procrastinating and complete your tasks.
- The skills taught by mindfulness can benefit everyone, especially those who suffer from ADHD. When you have a difficult task ahead of you, they can help you become calmer and more focused.

- Mindfulness practise can help you learn new skills and rewire your brain so that you no longer struggle. You will be able to improve your concentration, organisation, and self-motivation. Mindfulness will also help you improve your ability to self-observe and manage your attention.
- We understand that you are probably sceptical. You are most likely thinking positively for a few minutes each day, and the ADHD will disappear. No, not exactly. Sure, your meditation sessions will be important, and mindfulness will be used throughout the day, but these are long-term strategies. You will learn to practise mindfulness on your own by simply sitting in a quiet place where you will not be disturbed. You can start by focusing on the sensations of breathing in and out for five minutes. Pay close attention to how your stomach rises and falls. Do this every day for a few weeks, and you'll be able to increase your time to twenty minutes or more. You can do this before tests, before the next person in line to bat into gym class, or before meeting your friends for a social event that makes you nervous. The best part is that no one will ever know you're doing it.
- Remember that mindfulness can be practised while sitting or walking, so there are no obvious signs that you do so.
- You are just starting your journey to mindfulness meditation for ADHD, so don't be discouraged if it takes a few months to see real results.

Are you ready to make a positive change in your life and succeed? Let's get this party started!

Most likely, your ADHD isn't always a problem because you probably have times when it appears to be better than others. For example, you may discover that participating in your favourite sport, where you are constantly moving your body, is much easier for you than sitting through math class. Let's see if we can't figure out when and where your ADHD symptoms are causing you the most trouble. Make a note of your responses to these questions.

What do you consider to be the most severe symptom of your ADHD?

- Make a list of any situations that have exacerbated your symptoms.
- Is there anything that alleviates this symptom?
- Are there any changes you could make to minimise your symptoms in situations where your ADHD is more severe?
- Is there anything you could change in your environment to improve your symptoms?

It can be difficult to go through these difficulties, and you may feel that others have it easier than you. Consider a person who represents this and the difficulties they may be experiencing.

Everyone, including you, is a one-of-a-kind individual! Can you think of any talents or skills that make you a truly unique individual?

Yoga for ADD/ADHD

So you've decided to try mindfulness meditation and are curious about yoga. Yoga is all about slowing down and focusing, so this is an excellent choice! According to CHADD (2020), researchers have discovered that yoga practise can have positive effects on children and teens who have been diagnosed with ADHD — effects that last long after they leave the yoga mat for the day. These studies went on to discover that, when done twice a week, yoga can help reduce some of the symptoms associated with ADHD. The most noticeable difference was in the ability to pay attention in class and the improvement in-classroom skills. Yoga, in conjunction with mindfulness, can thus help teens with ADHD. There is no need to purchase any specialised equipment. A yoga mat is ideal if you want one. Aside from that, all you need are comfortable clothes and a quiet location. Alternatively, if you prefer to be in a group, you can find a yoga class to attend. You can find free online resources that provide exercises tailored to specific age groups.

According to the CHADD study (2020), if a parent and child practise yoga at the same time, they are more likely to strengthen each other's new habits. In addition, according to CHADD (2020), yoga has been shown to help improve ADHD symptoms. Practicing yoga moves for twenty minutes twice a week for eight weeks improved the subject's attention and focus testing. During your first yoga class, you may feel a variety of emotions and have varying levels of energy. You might, for example, feel supercharged with electricity. Yoga, like mindfulness exercises, requires you to concentrate on your breathing. In yoga, however, you will learn how to inhale and exhale during the execution of movements within a pose.

Yoga has additional advantages. It can help you boost your self-esteem, reduce stress, and even lose weight. Let's take a look at some yoga poses that are good for relaxing and expelling excess energy.

Pose as a tree. Because you must remain balanced while focusing, the tree pose is an excellent choice for working on focus and concentration. Begin by placing your palms together in front of your sternum, as if praying. Raise your palms and arms over your head while keeping your palms together and inhaling slowly. Exhale slowly and return your arms to their original position. Repeat this several times to improve your coordination between breaths and movement. When you've mastered this, you're ready to progress to the balancing portion of this exercise. Begin by concentrating on an immobile spot on the floor in front of you. Raise your left leg and place your left foot against the back of your right calf. Hold this pose for five breaths, then switch to the other side and repeat.

The cat-cow stance. Begin this yoga exercise by getting down on your hands and knees. You should keep your knees in line with your hips. Maintain a perpendicular relationship between your wrists, elbows, and shoulders, and the floor. Begin by inhaling and gradually rounding your spine in the direction of the ceiling. When you raise your back, your head drops, creating the silhouette of a startled cat. Hold that position for one second. Now exhale and return to your original starting position. On the following inhalation, lift your head, chest, and tailbone toward the ceiling, causing your back to curve down. You will also hold this pose for a single second before returning to your original position. Exhale. Repeat these positions for a total of ten times.

The forward bend while seated. Begin by sitting and extending your legs in front of you. Sit with good posture.

Lift your arms overhead as you inhale, then fold forward and reach for your toes as you exhale. Hold for ten seconds before returning to your starting position. Repeat ten times more.

The twist while seated. To begin, sit in a cross-legged position that is comfortable for you. Inhale deeply, then exhale while resting your right hand on your left knee. Gently twist your torso to the left while looking over your left shoulder, with your left hand behind your tailbone.

Hold for ten seconds before returning to your starting position. Rep this action in the opposite direction. You can repeat this setup up to ten times.

The lion is roaring. Simhasana (Lion's Breath) (sim-has-anna).

35

Because your posture resembles that of a lion, this has been dubbed "lion's breath." This practise is best done in the morning, but it can also be done in the evening if you allow 4 to 6 hours between your meal and this practise.

This is a fundamental yoga movement that helps to strengthen your throat, voice, and lungs. The lion pose is said to have numerous benefits, including stress and tension reduction, respiratory tract infection relief, and the treatment of stuttering, teeth grinding, and back pain. This is intended to be a fun exercise to keep you refreshed. Kneel on the floor and cross your ankles so that the front of the right ankle crosses over the back of the left ankle. Both sides of your feet must be pointed out. Place your hands on your knees, palms down, and spread your fingers apart while pressing firmly into your knees. While inhaling through your nose, open your mouth and stretch your tongue. Curl your tongue up toward your chin. For this, keep your eyes wide open and feel the muscles in the front of your throat contract. Exhale through your mouth, making a "ha" sound. To do this properly, your breath should pass over the back of your throat. Roar a few times in lion fashion, then reverse the orientation of your ankle cross and repeat.

The child's wide-knee pose. This is a relaxing pose that promotes relaxation. Anyone with a knee or hip injury should skip this one. Kneel on the floor and bring your big toes together. Exhale and lay your body onto your thighs, keeping your knees hip-width apart. Your hands should be beside you, palms facing up, pointing to the back of the room. This should help to relieve any shoulder tension. Your forehead should be on the ground, and you should gently roll your head from side to side while in this position. Slowly and steadily inhale and exhale.

Create your own yoga routine using your imagination. A deep breathing/yoga session once a day is a good way to start a new you. The more you practise, the faster you will integrate into your new routine and become more comfortable with the exercises. Don't have unrealistic expectations. Don't be discouraged if it takes some time for positive changes to occur. You are so daring to try new things!

If you have any questions about how to execute these poses, you can look at videos online. If you decide to look for a yoga class in your area, make sure to speak with the teachers involved because not all of them have experience working with people who have ADHD.

Meditation for ADHD:

Concentration, Feeling Overwhelmed, Patience, and Impulsiveness Guided Meditation #1 for Concentration

Welcome, This is the guided meditation for healing your lack of concentration. (10 seconds). Let's begin by finding a comfortable place to lie down or sit. (10 seconds). Turn off any devices that may distract you during this session and create a peaceful environment where you can be totally still. (10 seconds). You may wish to lie down and stretch out or sit in an upright position, whichever feels more comfortable for you. (20 seconds). Keep your eyes open for now and simply take a few deep breaths. (20 seconds).

Now, slowly close your eyes and as you do so, allow your breath to flow at its natural rhythm. (20 seconds). Notice how your body responds to each breath. (20 seconds). Feel the air as it flows through your nostrils and notice your chest as it rises and falls with each breath. (20 seconds). Focus on your stomach as it receives the warm air flowing through you. (20 seconds).

Allow your body to enjoy this moment of stillness as you relax. (20 seconds). Whenever you notice that the mind has wandered, simply bring your attention back to the breath. (20 seconds). Gently guide your mind back to your breath each time you feel it is moving away to something else. (20 seconds). No need to worry or feel you are doing anything wrong, just trust in yourself. (20 seconds). Continue to focus on your breath and see what else you notice about it, any sound that it makes, or how warm it feels. (20 seconds).

Listen to the air filling your lungs and then gradually expelling. (20 seconds). As you inhale, notice the air filling every fiber of your body with warmth and love. (20 seconds). Again, if you feel your mind wandering, simply bring it back to focus on your breath. (20 seconds). On the exhale, listen to the air as it passes through your mouth, like a soft breeze. (20 seconds). Your thoughts may be running here and there; that is perfectly natural. (15 seconds).

Simply bring your attention back to the sensations in your body as you inhale and exhale. (10 seconds). Allow your body to be still and release any tension. (20 seconds). Accept whatever sensations you may still be experiencing and just embrace this moment of calm. (15 seconds). We are not ready to begin our meditation session to help you with your concentration. (10 seconds).

Your lack of concentration prevents you from focusing because your mind is too busy. Today, we are going to learn how to quieten the mind, so that it does not disturb you. (20 seconds). Through practicing guided meditation regularly, you can train your mind to ignore distractions and bring its focus back to the present moment. (20 seconds). Your desire to be tranquil and calm is completely valid. (10 seconds). As you follow your breathing, notice the air entering your nose and flowing down to your chest and abdomen. (15 seconds). On the next inhale, hold the air inside for 3 seconds. 1, 2, and 3. (10 seconds). And now exhale slowly, allowing whatever tightness there is to be released. (20 seconds). Bring your attention to your body and notice any surface you are lying or sitting on. (20 seconds). Sense if the surface is soft, smooth, or hard, simply observe (30 seconds).

Notice your head resting on a pillow or on a mat. (15 seconds). Notice your back touching the chair or floor. (15 seconds). Notice your arms and legs, where they are resting. (15 seconds). Allow your body to explore these physical sensations. (20 seconds). Slowly turn your attention to one of these sensations. (20 seconds). Feel where your head is resting, or your hands. (20 seconds). You only need to focus on one area. (10 seconds). Gradually, turn your attention back to your breath. (20 seconds).

Notice how it ebbs in and out, bringing you total calm. (25 seconds). Follow your breath as it enters your body and focus on the place where it stops. (25 seconds). Perhaps your chest, or your abdomen. (20 seconds). You may notice it as it flows through your nostrils and down your throat. (20 seconds). Simply observe its sensation. (25 seconds). If your mind is beginning to wander, gently bring it back to your breath. (25 seconds). There is no need to force anything. Be gentle and caring with yourself. (15 seconds).

Slowly begin to count each breath as it rises and falls until you reach ten. (30 seconds). As you reach number ten, begin again, starting from one, and count each breath. 1, 2, and 3. Until you reach 10. (30 seconds). Each time your mind wanders, bring it gently back to your breath. (30 seconds). There is nothing else to do here, just breathe. (30 seconds). Allow random thoughts to come and go, like small birds fluttering in the sky. (25 seconds). Allow them to fly away as you maintain focus on your breath. (25 seconds). Notice one small thought as it flies through your mind. (10 seconds)

Now, slowly return your focus to your breath. (10 seconds). Stay in this calm, focused state for a while. (30 seconds). As you continue to breathe in and out, gradually bring your attention to the sensations of the surface where you sit or lie. (25 seconds). Allow your hands and feet to move lightly. (15 seconds) Now, on the count of three, slowly open your eyes. 1, 2, and 3. (15 seconds). Remain focused, calm, and relaxed throughout your day. (10 seconds)

Guided Meditation #2 for Feeling Overwhelmed

Welcome, This is a guided meditation to heal your feeling of being overwhelmed. (10 seconds). We will begin by getting you to breathe slowly and deeply, which will help you to relax as we continue this session. (10 seconds).

Try to find a comfortable space where you have room to lie down and stretch out. (10 seconds). If you prefer, you can remain seated. (10 seconds). Now gently close your eyes and as you do so, inhale deeply and hold until 3. 1, 2, and 3. (15 seconds). Now exhale slowly, releasing any tension as you do so. (15 seconds). Continue to inhale and exhale naturally, enjoying the sense of peace that comes with each breath. (10 seconds). Begin to create length in your spine by stretching. (20 seconds). Enjoy the lovely feeling that comes with your stretching. (10 seconds). Stretch and then relax. (10 seconds).

Scrunch up your shoulders for a count of 3. 1, 2, and 3. (15 seconds). Now soften your shoulders and feel all of that stress leave you. (10 seconds). Let your arms lie restfully by your side or on your lap. (20 seconds). As you inhale and exhale, feel each limb in your body softening. (20 seconds). Notice your arms and hands feeling soft and calm. (10 seconds). Fell how heavy your legs are, simply enjoying this moment. (10 seconds). Allow your stomach to relax. No need to hold anything in. (20 seconds).

Let the air flow through your rib cage and enjoy its calming energy. (20 seconds). Continue to inhale and exhale. (30 seconds). Slowly, calmly, with ease. (20 seconds). As you inhale, feel your lungs embracing each breath and filling you with a life-giving force. (20 seconds). Observe their slow movement in and out, in and out. (20 seconds). Enjoy this sensation of being here, at this moment, in total bliss. (20 seconds).

We will now begin with the process of relieving you of feeling overwhelmed. (15 seconds). Now is the time to let go of all the worry and stress you are carrying around with you. There are too many, and they are causing you to feel overwhelmed and unable to cope. (20 seconds).

The universe does not want you to feel like this and wishes you only peace and calm. (10 seconds). It's time to release the weight that you are carrying around with you and to feel light, free, and strong. (10 seconds). Let's begin by closing your eyes and taking a deep breath. (15 seconds). Nothing else is important at this moment in time. Simply your breath as it enters and leaves your body. (15 seconds). If your mind is still chattering away. Simply bring your attention to your breath and focus on that. Lower the volume on your mind, until you cannot hear it. (20 seconds). It is not necessary here to listen to your mind. Only the sound of the air flowing in and out of your lungs is important. (10 seconds). As each thought is created by the mind, continue to turn down the volume. They are still there, you just don't need to hear them now. (30 seconds). Allow yourself permission to experience total calm and peace. You deserve it. (30 seconds). Your mind is so busy doing what it needs to do that sometimes it forgets that you need calmness. (10 seconds). There is no blame or criticism here. Simply accept and continue to enjoy this peaceful moment. (20 seconds).

41

As you focus on the slow coming and going of your breath, your mind may want to get louder again, to remind you of all the things you need to do. (15 seconds).

Simply quieten those thoughts. You don't need to hear them now. (20 seconds). Inhale and listen to the cool air filling your lungs. Enjoy this lovely sensation. (20 seconds). On your exhale, again, notice the comforting sound of the air leaving you as it flows up into the air. (20 seconds). While enjoying each breath, I want you to focus on the soles of your feet. (20 seconds). Notice how relaxed your feet are, and how heavy they feel. (25 seconds).

As you focus, notice if your feet tingle or feel warm. Center your thoughts on them being grounded and at one with the universe. (25 seconds). Invite this comforting energy to slowly move up your legs, up to your abdomen and chest, finally reaching your shoulders, arms, and fingertips. (30 seconds). Observe the flow of energy through your body as it rises up your neck and to the top of your head. (25 seconds).

Continue to embrace each breath and welcome it into your body. (20 seconds). This is your sacred space, and you are grounded by warm energy. (20 seconds). Now you feel totally still, calm, and have no stress or tension. (10 seconds). Experience being present at this moment, like a tall tree in a beautiful meadow. (15 seconds). Notice the clarity of your being and the strength within you. (15 seconds). You are connected, grounded, and at one with the universe. (10 seconds). In your mind, see gentle rain falling from the sky. (10 seconds). It is falling on the tree in the meadow, bringing nourishment to every leaf and branch. (10 seconds). The soft rain falls on each leaf and the droplets are absorbed, allowing the tree to thrive and grow. (20 seconds). All of your negative energy is washed away by the gentle rain, leaving no trace of worry, stress, or fear. (20 seconds). Notice now how your whole body feels lighter, clearer, and stronger. (20 seconds). Your higher self has brought you clarity and peace. (10 seconds).

Clarity is a gift that helps you to make better decisions and regain harmony. You are full of harmony and balance. (20 seconds). As you return to this present moment, you feel light and carefree. (10 seconds).

Now you can turn the volume up slightly on your thoughts and not be overwhelmed by them. (20 seconds). Allow your mind to speak to you, but in a quiet tone, no need for too much noise and fuss. (15 seconds). Come back to your higher self through your breath whenever you feel that things are too much when you need clarity. (10 seconds). Slowly open your eyes. (10 seconds) Thank you and enjoy your day.

Guided Meditation #3 for Patience

Welcome, This is the guided meditation to help you to acquire patience. (10 seconds). First, find a quiet spot where you can make yourself comfortable. (20 seconds).

You can lay down or stay upright, whichever position feels the best for you at this moment. (10 seconds). Now close your eyes gently and take a nice deep breath in. (15 seconds), and as you breathe out, allow your whole body to soften and relax. (15 seconds).

On the next breath, breathe in through your nose for the count of four. 1, 2, 3, and 4. (20 seconds). Hold on to your breath for a count of five if you can. 1, 2, 3, 4, and 5. (10 seconds).

Then breathe out through your mouth up to 10. 6, 7, 8, 9, and 10 (20 seconds). Inhale again, 1, 2, 3, and 4. (15 seconds). Hold your breath. 1, 2, 3, 4, and 5. (10 seconds). Exhale out to 6, 7, 8, 9, and 10. (15 seconds). Continue this pattern of inhalation and exhalation one more time. (30 seconds).

Now allow your breath to return to its natural rhythm. (10 seconds). Notice how you are feeling after practicing these small, relaxing breaths. (15 seconds). Let your mind go to any physical sensation you are feeling at this moment. (15 seconds). Without judgment, just notice anything that is occurring within you. (10 seconds). Do you feel any pain, tension, discomfort? (10 seconds). Do you feel calm, relaxed, and safe? (10 seconds). Scan your body for anything that is attracting your attention and let it go. (10 seconds).

Today, you will allow your body to be free of any tension or stress. (10 seconds). Allow yourself to feel total serenity from head to toe. (10 seconds). We will now begin with the process of relieving you of your impatience. (15 seconds). It's normal to wish for everything in life to occur when you want it to, but your impatience is leaving you feeling frustrated, fatigued, and anxious. Perhaps you wish for the future to arrive sooner, or for people to behave differently.

All of this is impossible, and yet you allow yourself to be dictated to by your impatience. (20 seconds). Once you begin to accept and discipline your mind to be patient, you will remove those negative feelings of anger, anxiety, and stress. (10 seconds). You can begin today, at this moment. (10 seconds). Now that you are totally relaxed and comfortable, breathe in through your nose to a count of four. 1, 2, 3, and 4. (15 seconds). Hold your breath and on 4, release it through your mouth as you count to 5. 1, 2, 3, 4, and 5. (20 seconds). Breathe in again and count to 4. (15 seconds). Breathe out again and count to 5. (20 seconds). Repeat these patterns several times and then allow your breath to come and go at its own pace. (30 seconds).

Enjoy the feeling of being completely relaxed. (15 seconds). You are sitting on a warm, sandy beach on a sunny day. A small puppy is sitting at your feet. (20 seconds). You feel content and relaxed while the puppy plays with the sand. (20 seconds). At that moment, the puppy sees something on the beach and wants to run to chase it. (15 seconds). It is tugging at the leash, which is in your hand. (10 seconds).

The puppy is yelping excitedly and you have no idea what it has seen in the distance. (15 seconds). The puppy is tugging on the leash so strongly that it pulling on its neck. (10 seconds). You must get up and let the puppy led you to the focus of its attention. (15 seconds). After walking for just a few meters, you understand what it was that the puppy saw. (15 seconds). It is a bright red ball, and the puppy is delighted when you throw the ball and allow it to play. (15 seconds). You feel good because you were kind to the puppy and allowed it to run free and play with the ball. (10 seconds).

The pleasure that you receive fills you with happiness and joy. (10 seconds). Take a moment to observe how you feel in this moment. (15 seconds). As you continue to breathe in and out, notice what areas of your body feel anxious, stressed, or tense. (20 seconds). Go to an area that feels tense and focus on letting go.

Release the tension, just as you released the leash on the puppy. (15 seconds). Welcome more ease into your body and less tightness. (10 seconds). Embrace this experience of calm and tranquility. There is no led need to feel stress or anxiety. (20 seconds). Just as nature follows its own pace, life too has its own rhythm. You don't need to try to control it all the time. It is fine to let go. (15 seconds). Allow positive energy to fill you with each breath, and release all negative energy as you exhale.

Let go of whatever is keeping you in a state of anxiety and stress. (10 seconds). Just as the puppy pleases you; you can feel good about life once you learn to let go of impatient expectations and demands. (15 seconds). In the same way that the puppy has its nature, so too, life has its own ebb and flow. No need to force it. (20 seconds). Enjoy the feeling of slowing down and trying to resist. Simply trust that all things come in their own time. (20 seconds). Bring your awareness back to your body once more. (10 seconds). Inhale deeply and exhale slowly as you feel the positive energy inside you, filling your every sinew. (20 seconds).

Now that you have felt the beauty of letting go and being patient, trust in yourself to remain calm and stress-free at every moment. (15 seconds). When you are ready, slowly open your eyes. (10 seconds) Thank you for exploring patience with me.

Guided Meditation #4 for Impulsiveness

Welcome, This is the guided meditation for healing your impulsiveness. (10 seconds). So, let's begin by sitting in a comfortable position in a quiet space. (20 seconds). Remove anything that you feel may disturb you and switch off any devices. (20 seconds).

Allow your eyes to close and take a few deep breaths to settle you. (20 seconds). As your body begins to relax, inhale slowly and feel the air running through your nostrils and down into your lung. (20 seconds). Hold in the air until the count of 3 1, 2, and 3. (20 seconds), and now release slowly as you count 4, 5, and 6. (20 seconds).

On the next inhale, feel a warm glow spreading through your body, from your face down to your chest and stomach. (20 seconds), and now further down, to your legs, and onto your feet. (20 seconds). As you exhale, allow the breath to flow out, carrying with it any tension and worries that you may have. (15 seconds).

46

Follow the rhythm of your breathing and inhale slowly before exhaling. (10 seconds). Enjoy this sensation of calmness and relaxation. (25 seconds). If your mind jumps to any sensation or thought.

Simply let it be. (20 seconds). Gradually bring your focus back to the warm sensation of serenity that you feel. (20 seconds). Release any troubling thoughts as you slowly exhale and let them disappear into the atmosphere. (15 seconds). Relax your brow, your jawline, and your mouth. (20 seconds). Scrunch your shoulders a little and then let them drop. (15 seconds). Sense the calmness as you continue to inhale and exhale. (30 seconds). Allow your stomach to relax and let your arms rest on your lap. (20 seconds).

Feel your legs and feet enjoying the sensation of being grounded on the floor. (20 seconds). As you continue to sit here, remember that there is no need to do anything other than enjoy this serene state. (20 seconds). Invite the sense of peace to envelop you in a warm, safe place. (20 seconds). We will now begin with the process of relieving you of your impulsiveness. (15 seconds). I want you to focus on your tendency to be impulsive, which can lead you to make bad decisions that have negative outcomes. (10 seconds).

When you act impulsively, you may put yourself or others at risk because you behave without giving yourself the time to think things through. (15 seconds) You need to achieve clarity and patience, and to believe in your own judgment, not rely on your impulses, which may get you into trouble. (15 seconds). While you are relaxing, I want you to follow your breath as it flows in and out. (20 seconds). There is nothing else to do here. Simply relax and be in the moment. (15 seconds).

As your body becomes still, notice any sensations, but no need to react to them. Simply observe. (20 seconds) You may feel irritated, anxious, confused, all sensations are acceptable. (20 seconds). While your body is totally still, turn your attention to your mind. (10 seconds). There is no need to react to anything, just observe any thoughts that are occurring while you continue to feel relaxed. (20 seconds) You don't need to judge yourself or criticize any aspect of this moment. (20 seconds). As each thought arises, release it as you exhale. (20 seconds).

It is a gentle process, exhale and release. (15 seconds). If you feel distracted by a noise in the room or a smell, gently bring your mind back to your breath. (20 seconds). No need to pay attention to any thoughts popping up. Simply allow them to come and go. (20 seconds). By observing your mind without feeling the need to react, you can avoid any impulses that may be pressing you to do this or that. (20 seconds). At this moment, you don't need to do absolutely anything. Simply be present and calm. (25 seconds). I want you to focus on your chest or stomach area while breathing steadily, direct your breath to that area on the inhale. (20 seconds). In doing so, thank yourself for being patient, calm, and sure of your judgment. (25 seconds). Center your mind on your chest or stomach and notice any sensations. Do you feel a tightness or something you can't explain? Stay with the sensation until it passes, breathe out, and release it. (20 seconds).

You may experience waves of pent-up frustration, anger, or irritability. These are all perfectly normal. (10 seconds). When you focus on where those negative feelings are coming from, you can simply breathe and exhale, allowing them to leave you. (20 seconds). Take another deep breath in and embrace the sense of clarity that you experience now. (20 seconds). Slowly come back to where you are at this moment. (10 seconds). Notice that your mind is also becoming more alert to your surroundings. (10 seconds).

Stretch your arms and legs and check the sensation of being calm and rested. (15 seconds). Slowly raise your eyelids and let your

48

eyes focus. (10 seconds). Store this feeling of being in control within your memory and come back to it the next time you feel the desire to act impulsively. (20 seconds). You now have perfect control over your behavior and actions. (10 seconds). Thank you for joining in this meditation.

Exercise in Centering Meditation for Calm and Focus

It is critical to practise how to achieve a relaxed state of comfort and concentration. This should be done on a daily basis. It is critical to be able to sit in inner stillness and focus on your deepest feelings. When learning this, keep in mind that working with a younger child usually results in more nervous body movements. That's all right. Allow it to be as it is and work on it

49

patiently by focusing on breathing. Make it a game for children to close their eyes for short periods of thirty seconds to a minute at a time.

Adults should start with two to three minutes of exercise.

1. Pay attention to the colours you see when you close your eyes.

2. Visualize the centre of the space you perceive and gently focus on it.

3. Take three slow, deep breaths through your nose and say Ah-hum three times with feeling. These sounds elicit a happy feeling in the nervous system and mean "I am." Consider the Ah sound on the inhale and the hum on the exhale during both inhalation and exhalation. Consider whether you can feel the vibrations of these sounds.

This technique teaches you how to self-manage and be at ease in a relaxed state, allowing your system to be more receptive.

Step 1: Take a comfortable seat and close your eyes. Concentrate on the centre of the blue-black space you see when you close your eyes.

Step 2: Inhale deeply through the nose and hold for a few seconds before exhaling even more slowly than you inhaled. Feel the breath moving through your nasal passageway and into your lungs. Consider your breath filling your entire body.

Step 3: As you continue to be aware of your breathing, imagine it in a different colour.

Consider inhaling and exhaling the coloured breath.

Step 4: After a minute or two, add a mantra, which is a sound vibration that helps to focus the mind. Repeat inwardly, Ah Hum, with your eyes closed and your body relaxed. This means that I am. When heard, the enunciation of Ah Hum creates a resonance of delight. The sound vibration clears stress-induced plaque from the nervous system, allowing it to open, relax, and focus. Simply sit for the allotted time, then repeat the process.

Step 5: If thoughts arise, simply observe them and remind yourself, "I am not that thought." That thought is known to me."

Then repeat the mantra, Ah Hum. Spend at least seven minutes meditating.

The Laughter Release Exercise

Laughing is one of the quickest ways to replace negative internal dialogue and restore balance to a stressed system. Laughter triggers powerful neurological and biochemical processes in the brain and nervous system, which boosts your overall well-being.

Laughter rejects the seriousness you are imbuing on your thoughts and frees you from the hypnotic spell you have placed on them.

Step 1: Stand in front of a mirror or in a circle with others and say aloud, "Begin laughing." Use your inner child to think of silly things, make silly faces, do something silly, or laugh for no reason. Have some fun! Be outrageous, outrageous, and completely insane! Have a good time with it, even if your laughter is forced at first. Continue to do so. Make a fool of yourself until you make it! Laugh at how awkward or self-conscious you feel as a result of doing this.

Step two. When you stop laughing, tell yourself, "Keep laughing." Make it enjoyable and do it for at least two minutes!

This tool is great for releasing tension and shifting any seriousness in your self-talk. Each burst of "Ha ha ha ha ha!" sets off a chain reaction of relaxing neurotransmitters that will assist you in regaining your focus.

The Ending

Wrap your arms around your body, squeezing tight with love and care. Maintain a firm grip and a cheerful demeanour. "I am blessed with life," say aloud. Thank you (God, life, creation, and so on)."

Visualization of a Safe Location

It is extremely helpful to know that you can access places in your mind to feel safe, protected, and grounded in order to maximise present attentiveness. Life's harsh realities can be overwhelming at times, making it difficult to maintain a state of presence. The goal of the safe place visualisation is to allow you to disassociate and find greater peace and comfort within your mind at any time. There may be bursts of instability while distressing influences are addressed for correction. When old patterns are deconstructed, it is common for people to feel befuddled. The known gives way to the unknown.

The first step

What follows should be recorded in a gentle tone on your smartphone or a recorder. You might want to listen to some soothing music while reading this for added comfort. Slowly and with feeling, read these lines.

Please take a few moments to slowly and easily breathe. Simply relax and feel at ease in your current situation. Close your eyes and take a few moments to relax while taking a few slow deep breaths and settling into a comfortable position. Allow your mind to wander back to a time when you felt safe and protected while out in nature. It could be a place you've visited or one you've always wanted to visit. Please relax and allow whatever images, even if they are unexpected, to arise. Pay attention to the amount of light in your images, noting whether it was dim or bright. Is there anything else you remember hearing in the background? Take note of how you feel as you observe the images and details that come to your attention.

Breathe easily and freely, feeling safe and protected as your body relaxes deeper with each breath. With each breath, you become more immersed in this special place, which becomes indelible in your memory. Are you aware of what the temperature was at the time you were in this location? What thoughts come to mind when you're in this relaxed and safe environment? Is it audible? Are there any colours that stand out more than others? How is your breathing going while you're in this safe haven? Take a few moments to simply observe the colours in whatever image you are aware of. Investigate the location of the image and how you feel while there. In an unforgettable way, breathe and embody the comfort and relaxation of being there. Stay in this state for as long as you want, remembering that you can return to it at any time. Feel the statement "I am safe, I am at ease" deeply.

Consider what comes to mind when you think of an icon that represents this safe haven. It could be a particular tree, the sun, a flower, or some other symbol that you associate with peace and safety. It could just be a specific statement. Whatever it is, become aware of it so that you can be drawn back into this safe and protected place whenever you think of it, feeling the comfort and ease of being there in an instant. Stay as long as you want, and when you're ready to reconnect with your surroundings, remember the symbol or statement that represents this space, knowing you can easily and quickly return to this space whenever you want.

Step 2: Listen to your recording in a quiet place where you won't be disturbed. Listen as often as you want, but especially when you need a safe place to be.

Step 3: When you emerge from this internal journey, look for the image, statue, icon, or other item that represented safety to you. If you want, you can draw something. Display two of these symbols around you in places you see frequently throughout the day, such as by your computer or bed.

Identifying an Empowering Model

Developing focus entails giving your mind a clear direction as to what you want to concentrate on. It is especially important to have a right-minded reference system in place to assist you in evaluating any situation in which you find yourself. Personal guidelines will influence how you perceive and act in the world.

A personal code brings order to the constant external chaos in order to process the never-ending flow of information. This establishes a model of self-reliance, self-containment, and self-awareness that you strive to emulate.

Step 1. Make a list of two or three people you admire and believe can serve as positive role models for you in your own life.

Step 2: Write down the characteristics you notice in these role models to specify what you admire about them.

54

Step 3: Make a list of how your models handle personal, interpersonal, physical, emotional, mental, and spiritual aspects of life. What are their perspectives? How do they carry their bodies? How do they walk, treat others, talk to themselves internally, find motivation, use different coping strategies, and so on? Put yourself in the shoes of the person being modelled; pretend to be them and walk in their shoes. Take note of how you mimic what they do.

Step 4: Investigate their internal processing: Inquire about the criteria they use when making a decision. What resources do they draw on, both within themselves and from others? Do they have a support group that they hang out with? Friends? Professionals? What are their physical, mental, emotional, and spiritual disciplines? Do they have back-up plans or conditional goals in place if the current ones don't work out? Do they have a plan for exiting the company? What kind of troubleshooting methods do they employ to investigate failed ventures? This process will reveal the numerous gaps in how your role model actually lives in the world. Once any discrepancies are discovered, you can conduct additional research into the specifics of your models. It's critical to distinguish between your model's social projection and their underlying private personalities. It helps you accept your flaws by removing the masks of perfection that your heroes work hard to maintain. Discovering the struggles your role models had to overcome in order to achieve their level of success gives you more compassion for your own struggles and those who are a part of them.

Step 5: For at least one day, pretend to be one of your role models. Take note of the changes and adjustments you must make to your attitude and habits in order to behave as they would. Finally, consider what traits/qualities/attributes of theirs you would like to emulate. This will aid in the development of your personal code.

55

CHAPTER 3.

SUCCESS STORIES OF PEOPLE WITH ADHD

This disorder affects a large number of people, including many well-known personalities.

It has been regarded as an anomaly by some, but in other cases, given the difficulties they have had to face and overcome, it has allowed them to develop other types of characteristics such as greater creativity, even providing positive reinforcement to their personalities in the long run.

In this section, we will discuss 12 famous people who have or are suffering from ADHD.

Tatum, Channing

Channing Tatum is now a big-budget movie star. He is well-known internationally and is admired by many people all over the world. His most well-known films include 21 Jump Street, The Vow, Magic Mike, and Dear John. Channing's best qualities are his good looks, sense of humour, and dance abilities. As you can see, Channing was once diagnosed with ADHD, but it is no longer obvious.

During interviews, he expresses his desire to overcome his condition. However, with proper treatment and management, he has become one of Hollywood's most prominent figures. Channing stated that he used to feel very different when he was around normal kids, but that did not stop him from pursuing his dreams.

Timberlake, Justin

Justin Timberlake is a well-known singer and songwriter from the United States. Apologize and Sexy Back are two of his most well-known songs. Justin stated in one interview that he was diagnosed with ADHD as well as OCD. This condition is more difficult to manage because it combines two distinct behavioural issues. Despite the obstacles, he was tenacious in his pursuit of the spotlight, and he was successful.

Phelps, Michael

This may truly astound you. Michael Phelps holds the record for the most medals won in Olympic history.

Michael's teachers were unhappy with his behaviour when he was in elementary school. He was said to have difficulty sitting still in his chair.

He was always moving around and making a lot of noise. His parents were concerned by his behaviour, so they took him to the doctor. He was diagnosed with ADHD at that time.

With 28 medals from the Olympic Games, he is the most successful Olympic athlete in history. During a press conference, the famous swimmer revealed that he was diagnosed with ADHD as a teen. Despite being told by one of his teachers that he would never accomplish anything significant in his life, he used swimming as a form of therapy for his disorder, and the results have gone down in world sports history.

His parents attempted to treat his condition with medications.

However, they only served to stigmatise Michael, so they decided to discontinue his medications. Instead of using drugs, Michael concentrated on swimming. This has helped him focus and be more disciplined. Michael eventually rose to become the world's best swimmer.

Levine, Adam

Who hasn't heard of Adam Levine? Of course, you've seen him on TV and may have noticed some odd behaviour whenever the camera rolls. These actions and attitudes are not always deliberate. They are occasionally signs and symptoms of his ADHD.

Adam is the lead singer for the well-known band Maroon 5. He is also well-known for his role as a judge on the popular TV show The Voice. Adam's condition is easier to manage now that he was diagnosed with ADHD at a young age. As a result, he was able to take the necessary medications and therapies to keep him healthy.

Despite these efforts, he occasionally exhibits the various signs and symptoms of ADHD. He stated that recording music could be difficult at times. Despite this, he did not give up and has inspired many people to never give up on their dreams.

Paris Hilton

Paris Hilton is a well-known actress, model, and television host. During an interview with Larry King, Paris admitted to having ADHD. She stated that she has been taking medications since the age of 12. She had a lot of trouble concentrating at first, but she has learned how to control it. Paris stated that everything is now back to business, and she is doing well in her business and entertainment careers.

As you can see, the majority of the celebrities mentioned above stated that dealing with ADHD is extremely difficult at first. However, with the right treatment and approaches, you and your child will be able to overcome it sooner or later. Some symptoms may reappear at a later age, but fighting the condition will be easier. These examples may inspire you and your child as you learn to manage and overcome ADHD.

Biles, Simone

It was the same American gymnast and Olympic champion who stated that she had been taking pharmaceutical drugs for ADHD since she was 19 years old. She was also found positive in doping tests several times as a result of her treatment.

This athlete is the exception to the rule, teaching the world a valuable lesson: even in a sport requiring extreme concentration and application, ADHD is not a barrier to success.

Ryan Gosling's

The famous Canadian actor, star of films such as "Noah's Diary," "Drive," and "La La Land," has been diagnosed with ADHD since he was a child. Because he couldn't read, he had a lot of trouble at school, which led to bullying incidents.

Stallone, Sylvester

During his childhood, the iconic action movie actor and unforgettable performer of Rocky and Rambo in their respective sagas experienced several problematic school episodes that resulted in his expulsion from more than 14 schools. He was a wild child who was restless due to his ADHD. Despite his disorder, he went on to become a movie icon.

Jordan, Michael

The most famous basketball player of all time has had ADHD since he was a child. Because of his obvious lack of concentration, several doctors and teachers told his parents that he would not have many professional and work opportunities because of his hyperactivity. He is currently regarded as one of the greatest athletes and champions in history.

Usain Bolt's bio

Once again, an Olympic athletic icon. One of the most surprising cases is that of a Jamaican sprinter. The world record holder had a difficult childhood because he was a restless and hyperactive adolescent, which influenced his upbringing. Again, ADHD was not an issue, as he was able to find his escape and expression through athletics and speed.

Mr. Bill Gates

The computer mogul, co-founder of Microsoft, and one of the world's wealthiest people. He was an intensely curious child who would not stop asking questions about anything that piqued his interest from a young age. Later, due to his lack of academic performance as a result of ADHD, he was forced to drop out of Harvard University, but this did not prevent him from establishing his own company and launching Windows in 1985.

Walt Disney Jr.

As a boy, the famous creator of movies and animated characters we love suffered from severe concentration problems.

He preferred to spend his time drawing and daydreaming, which led many of his peers to label him as "weird." He devoted himself to newspaper distribution, which had a negative impact on his academic performance. Because of the difficulties and distractions caused by his disorder, he was also fired from several jobs in communication and media.

Christie, Agatha

61

Since childhood, the successful British mystery writer has been labelled as the "slowest" member of her family. She was not only diagnosed with dyslexia, but also with ADHD, and she struggled with both disorders throughout her life.

Despite her poor handwriting, her works were read all over the world, and she became one of the most famous writers of all time.

J.Law

One of the world's highest-paid young actresses, with an Oscar for one of her performances. Her childhood, on the other hand, was far from idyllic: before being diagnosed with ADHD, she was dubbed "nitro" (nitroglycerin) at school due to her constant hyperactivity.

Hamilton, Lewis

The British Formula One driver was the youngest person to win a World Cup, matching Michael Schumacher's record of seven championships. Hamilton was a rambunctious and disobedient child who was later diagnosed with ADHD. However, it was clear to him from the moment he drove his first kart at the age of six that he wanted to devote himself to the world of motor racing, and his restlessness or lack of concentration in other areas did not stand in his way.

ADHD in Real Life Personal Narratives and Experiences

Janelle—Fitness Trainer

I prefer to work in children's fitness because it keeps me more active and engaged. I am currently teaching children's exercise classes, but I am having difficulty in my managerial role. I work as a sales and facilities manager, balancing staff scheduling, customer service, facility and equipment maintenance, and teaching classes, which is my favourite part of my job.

At the age of 24, I discovered I had ADHD. I didn't find out until it was too late because I did well in school. I was a mediocre student. I had a tendency to "fly under the radar." In school, I went unnoticed and was labelled as shy or lost in my own world. In school, I doodled a lot and did not take any honours courses. I know I could have pushed myself harder, but I didn't have the motivation.

In college, it was the same. I was a mediocre student. Despite having poor test results, I completed all of my assignments on time (which is unusual for someone with ADHD!).

After graduating from college, I began working full-time or on weekends. That's where the problems started. I worked as a summer camp counsellor, which I thoroughly enjoyed, but as I advanced to higher positions at a recreation centre, I found it difficult to recall tasks assigned to me by the manager.

I'd also been demoted from a couple of jobs because I couldn't recall the step-by-step procedures for opening and closing recreation centres. I recall being shown multiple times how to close sales batches, lock up, and so on, but I couldn't do it in the time frame they required, so I was fired. I failed time and again, even when told the same thing over and over when I couldn't understand it.

When I had the "Aha!" moment, I understood and excelled. When I started getting demoted from job to job, I knew something wasn't right. I realised I did what was required of me, but I never went above and beyond or requested additional tasks. When I spoke with a coworker at the time, he mentioned that he was on medication for ADHD.

I inquired about it, as well as how he knew since I was experiencing symptoms. He claimed to be hyperactive, which I did not believe.

I looked up ADHD on the internet and realised I might be the Inattentive type. I began attending weekly therapy sessions to learn about ADHD and decided to get tested.

My findings included some observations made by my mother when I was a child, such as "underperforming for people she didn't like" or "pretending not to know things to gain special attention." I also left my room in a state of disarray, procrastinated on schoolwork, and forgot to pick up something for a project until the day before. I also admitted to feeling "dumb" or "failure" and experiencing extreme anxiety before and after work/school.

The results of the tests confirmed severe signs in all executive functioning domains, as well as low scores in perceptual reasoning, despite being in the 96th percentile for processing speeds listed on the Adult Intelligence Scale. I then began taking stimulant medication and going to therapy, which helped me excel at my next job as a Children's Fitness Instructor and even get promoted to a manager position.

When I'm bored (which is frequently), I get creative. I come up with creative ways to have fun, especially during this quarantine we're currently experiencing. I've made a home zoo, a home concert, a scavenger hunt, a theme park, a beauty salon, and other things. In addition, I have several solutions to a problem. There is never a single correct answer.

What I like best about myself, and what my friends like best about me (sometimes), is that I don't mince words. Even if it appears simple, I make observations right away. For example, a coworker (now a close friend) was new to working with me, and I asked her why she wasn't wearing a wedding ring if she was married. It was a standard question to me, but it was an invasion of privacy to someone else.

Even if it appears differently to others, they understand I'm not implying anything. I enjoy observing things and learning new things. I'm always asking questions and trying to figure out what's going on around me.

The most difficult challenge for me is always starting a new job or moving up in my current position. I am constantly anxious and under pressure to perform like a "normal" person in order to succeed or risk being demoted again. I often feel as if I need to change my personality and conform in order to succeed. I usually don't tell employers or employees about my ADHD because I believe it affects my ability to get a job, despite the fact that we are supposedly "protected" by the Americans with Disabilities Act. It's a harsh world, and I don't want to be perceived as such.

I tried to keep my ADHD to myself, but I realised that it's a part of me that others must accept. My mother was fine with it, but my father was furious when we got the test results.

"There's nothing wrong with her; she doesn't need any kind of pills!" he insisted. I've told a few close friends, and they agree. They understand my straightforward but silly personality and, in any case, they adore me for it.

Because of the ADHD stigma, I rarely tell anyone at work. One of the children we teach, for example, frequently exhibits symptoms.

According to one coworker, "He has ADHD, and no one can keep this kid under control. He has problems, and I can't stand him. I hear statements like that all the time, so I spoke up and said, "So what?" I suffer from ADHD. You must figure out what he is interested in and make it a fun challenge for him. He'll be more involved."

I've also had to confess to a coworker because she was harassing me at work, accusing me of being slow and asking what was wrong with me when I was trying to count office inventory and making mistakes. When did I tell her I was hoping for sympathy? Instead, I received, " "h. formalised I had a feeling something was wrong with you."

I mentioned it to my boss. He had no idea at the time, but my coworker spilled the beans and revealed my personal information to him. "Janelle told me she has ADHD, we need to discuss this ASAP and figure out what to do with her," I read in a text message that included another staff member. It was an invasion of privacy and a violation of my human rights. They questioned why I hadn't informed them sooner, and I told them the truth. I didn't expect to be hired, so I tried to blend in with everyone else. I didn't think it was a big deal, but it was to them.

I enjoy playing video games because they can hold my attention for several hours. I also enjoy watching TV and playing the piano (when I'm motivated enough to start practising). Hiking and Ultimate Frisbee are two of my favourite outdoor activities.

Michelle Obama's Let's Move! health campaign to reduce childhood obesity has a special place in my heart. I am an active person who enjoys outdoor activities and adventures. I despise how much screen time has taken over our lives and enjoy unplugging every now and then. I also majored in Parks and Recreation in college, and I want children and adults to value the environment more and care for it before it is lost to future generations.

Josh—Director of Research

I was always a good student in high school and elementary school, which is a typical ADHD story. I did well in discussions, you know, the main point of what was going on. But I never ever turned in my homework. I don't recall ever doing homework. Until I was about 15 years old, I had never read anything.

And if you go back even further, to fifth grade in elementary school. We used to sit in these groups of tables, and my teacher moved me to a different group so that I would stop talking. Then she moved me from that cluster to another, and I still wouldn't stop talking. Then she moved me to my own cluster as if I wasn't with other people, and I still wouldn't stop talking. Then she turned me around so I was facing the wall, and it just kept going like that.

What happened was that I took the ACT and did well on the math and scientific reasoning sections, which are like reading charts and visual stuff. So, I got like, wow, you can get into any engineering programme you want on math. And then on the reading test, I scored like; did you even fill out this whole thing? So, at that point, the school suggested a psych evaluation to see if there was a learning disability present.

Following that, I was prescribed stimulant medication by a psychiatrist. I took it briefly but then stopped. I finally went back to see a therapist, and then a psychiatrist, almost 20 years later. It took me over a year to be honest with the therapist and tell him I had previously been prescribed a stimulant. I was prescribed medication as soon as I did, and it was fantastic. After two days, I had read an entire page of a book without repeating a single

67

sentence. Then I got six pages and actually read them all without getting distracted.

Because of the social stigma associated with ADHD, I had put off talking to my psychiatrist about it. I was afraid that bringing up attention or activation symptoms would make me appear to be a drug seeker. It didn't feel right.

My therapist and psychiatrist did not investigate ADHD as a possible diagnosis because I have a successful career, am a good parent, and am very analytical and articulate.

I began learning a lot more about what ADHD was. I'd never read about an illness of any kind that I felt so strongly connected to in terms of any possible experience I'd had. And just explaining parts where I felt I was different, or whatever, and it was all starting to make sense. Yeah. I mean, I'm sure almost any adult who's been diagnosed with this has had a life experience, and then all of a sudden, wow, it's all coming together.

It's as if to say, "Wow!" It all comes together, and you're left wondering, "Why did I take so long?" It took so long because I was seeing a marriage therapist, a therapist for myself, and a psychiatrist, and I tried to be honest with all of them, but I wasn't. I mean, I wasn't clearly describing all of the ADHD symptoms I have. They look at me as if to say, "Oh, everyone has this, everyone procrastinates." Everyone, you know, suffers from inattention or a lack of working memory.

But the point is that I avoided looking into ADHD because of the stigma, and then when I brought it up with my therapist or other people, they just kind of dismiss it because it's as if they look at it and say, okay, Josh, you run a business.

I've been working on simple coping skills since I was about 13 years old. I always, literally always, have a pen and a notebook with me. I've always had it because I know, and I'm not sure why, but I don't have any working memory. It's gone if I don't write it down within a minute. I can't have this conversation without looking at notes, and it's just that I need to be able to draw a picture. I need to be able to write something down or else I won't be able to collect my thoughts later. I've had a lot of lists to keep me organised. I externalise whatever it was that was supposed to be my brain.

I have strange things I'm really good at and strange things I'm really bad at, and the way I compensate is really interesting. I don't have a strong episodic memory. For example, I can't recall any events, content, or knowledge. But I remember trends, and I can easily see how one concept can evolve into another.

As a result, I believe it is due to ADHD. I believe what I've done is that I can't hold the memory, so I remember the type of rule that was used to go from this one to that one. I only have about 60 rules that I follow all the time, but I don't have a thousand memories that I need to remember.

Rejection sensitivity dysphoria, as well as emotional dysregulation, struck me hard. When someone says, "Yeah, aren't we all a little ADHD?" this thing, combined with all the other symptoms, makes them think, "Yeah, aren't we all a little ADHD?"

Yeah, isn't emotional dysregulation a b*tch? They, as you know, do not have that experience as people with ADHD; they do not have rejection sensitivity and emotional dysregulation to the extent that ADHD people do.

So I got my Ph.D. in engineering and worked with my advisor, with whom I got along well. He had feelings for me, you know. He stated that I was the best student he had ever had. We had one conversation in which he was disappointed with me and became frustrated; I believe he was just having a bad day and was frustrated, and I said something that irritated him because he was angry about something else. And it took me 18 months to recover from that when it happened to me. I finished my degree as soon as I could because it had destroyed me.

I could tell you a million more stories. There have been so many other things that have occurred. Our relationship is fine, and I know I can look back on it now and understand what happened, as well as look back on the specific episode and not be as angry about it. I can be less angry or hurt about it and still understand where he was coming from.

I would prefer not to have ADHD. I have the impression that I am playing life on hard mode. Emotional dysregulation is a nightmare. It's extremely embarrassing not to be able to read or do mental arithmetic. However, I believe that some aspects of my personality that I like about myself are a result of ADHD. I am a very active and enthusiastic person.

My "contagious enthusiasm" is always noticed and appreciated. I'm a driven individual, and it shows. Many of these characteristics are shared by people who have ADHD.

People in my field are asking me, "How is this guy so enthusiastic about what we do?" I remember working with the engineers and asking them, "Do you understand what we get to do?" Do you realise that we have a skill set that allows us to solve or address issues that other people do not have? We get to have fun in this area, and I just go on and on about it, and I talk about the field that I work in, and it's like, this is so amazing, and I'm like, wow, I love this. I get so animated and excited that people think I'm hilarious. This is unbelievable.

I'm the boss, so I'm like the guy in the field who other people in other companies want to listen to. Josh, for example, is going to give a webinar. We'll have to call in on this one. It's going to be fantastic because I get so animated. I gave a webinar to a few hundred people on Wednesday morning. When I get excited about something, I go completely insane.

People with ADHD are always talking about hyper-focus and perseverance, and this is essentially where my entire career has come from. I can basically only focus on one thing at a time. I do that for a week straight, and whatever comes out at the end is usually pretty good. That's one part of it. But the issue is that almost every time I do that, I'm working on something that isn't a critical path. This isn't what I'm supposed to be doing. It's attempting to avoid something else.

You know, this is just me getting excited about something and diving into it whether or not it's what I'm supposed to do. I take a lot of other things that should happen and don't do them. I've always thought about it, and the language I've used to describe it is hiding.

Because of my ADHD, I have many quirks that people find endearing. I spend a lot of time talking to myself. I forget things and make mistakes, and I take it for granted. Everyone knows I always have a pen on me. At all times, I carry at least two pens and two notebooks (one is very small and the other is in my wallet).

But if I had to choose between being a passionate person and losing my emotional dysregulation, rejection sensitivity dysphoria, and ability to read, I'd gladly be a passionless bore. Just give me my books and leave me alone.

I quickly become depressed. I never get depressed or angry. When I'm angry, I have tunnel vision. On the other hand, when I'm happy, I'm absurdly (and possibly irritatingly) happy. In my line of work, this is referred to as "infectious enthusiasm."

Procrastination and hyperfocus/perseverance This sums up my professional life. I only work on things that are absolutely necessary and have passed their deadline. By becoming completely absorbed in non-critical path work, I avoid working on things.

When I get a new problem to work on, I only work on that problem. For a very long time. Days, at times. I am unable to read. I had a reading tutor in elementary school but stopped because my parents didn't prioritise it. I hadn't read a book until I was 15 years old (even a picture book). I do not suffer from dyslexia or any other learning disability (I was tested). Because I have a limited working memory, it is difficult for me to internalise anything as I read. Instead of continuing, each sentence makes me think of something else. Because I'm impatient with my reading speed, I skip over words.

Attention/concentration issues At any given time, I'm only taking in about 10% of what's in front of me. I become distracted, bored, or fixate on the first part of what happened and ignore the rest. I don't see the big picture like other people. I'll have to make up for the time I've missed. Through very strong deductive reasoning skills, I've become very good at making up the other pieces. But the "gist" can only take me so far. My episodic memory is extremely untrustworthy.

I'm a tad impatient. Many people describe me as being patient. I may appear patient on the outside, but most of the time I'm just incredibly frustrated and impatient.

My wife is the most influential in terms of how other people react to my ADHD. We were already having a lot of problems with our marriage. We haven't been anywhere close to "happily married" in years.

She got the book "Is It You, Me, or Adult ADHD" from a friend after I told her about ADHD. She had a strong connection to the book. So much so that she believed that all of the therapy we'd been working on had been counterproductive. We've been apart since the diagnosis, and I believe it's because of it.

Several of my friends and family members are doctors. When I told them, they laughed and called me a liar. They easily dismiss my professional success. They lack the necessary domain knowledge. It's still unpleasant.

I told a few of my friends that I have ADHD. Some say, "don't we all?" while others are more supportive. I haven't told anyone at work because I'm afraid of being judged. Spending time with my family is a simple pleasure for me. I'm having fun with my kids. Movies are being watched.

When I have some alone time, I enjoy engineering mathematics. It used to be more enjoyable for me. I enjoy it when I can do it. My ability fluctuates according to my mood. This is where hyper-focus really comes into play. I can spend weeks drilling on a fun math problem.

I am deeply committed to civil rights in general. I donate to Planned Parenthood, the ACLU, the Human Rights Campaign, and the International Rescue Committee on a regular basis. I worked in community organising for several years. From assisting neglected public housing tenants in forming building associations and campaigning for local government officials to picking up trash and driving people to vote, there is something for everyone.

In addition, I am very enthusiastic about my field of expertise and science/engineering education in general. I study a field that is not covered in any engineering undergraduate curriculum but is present in every application of materials manufacturing. My passion has evolved into raising awareness and engaging undergraduates.

Andrea is a Licensed Social Worker and an Interior Designer

I am the mother of four adult children, the majority of whom live elsewhere. I've always struggled with restlessness, easily boredom, a need for a lot of stimulation and activity, poor concentration, impulsive blurting out of answers at school, talking during class, and not paying attention. I was chastised for moving my feet around too much on the desk in front of me.

I did well in school overall, but I was frequently in trouble, which was due in part to my ADHD and in part to my home environment. The majority of it is due to ADHD. I couldn't concentrate if I was bored. I rushed through work, attempting to complete projects that did not require planning anything in a step-by-step manner. I was impatient with slow work or reading and craved constant action.

When I was required to read something, if it didn't interest me, I couldn't. I'd read the same paragraph over and over again and still had no idea what it said or who was who in the story. I wasn't paying attention because my mind kept wandering to more pressing matters. All of this was compounded by the anxiety and stress in my home, which may have set me up. However, that symptom persisted in my house.

When I worked in retail, I was embarrassed by how long my line grew and how slow my checkout was. Each item's price had to be entered manually. Because barcodes had not yet been invented, I had to type the price and department number without

74

transposing the numerals and remember the digits for each price so I could type it in.

I was taken off the register and eventually fired because I was having difficulty initiating the actions I was supposed to take, namely organising the hardware department's stock room. Looking at the massive stack of boxes and inventory, I had no idea where to put anything or how to organise it.

In high school, I was becoming dissatisfied with the adult responsibilities that were looming, such as doing my taxes, keeping track of mail, and staying organised.

I couldn't find my niche as a college student and was easily bored by tedious projects. I switched majors several times, including once when I had to type papers. I didn't have a computer; instead, I used a typewriter, and if I made a mistake, I had to start over. We were only allowed a few typos, even with White Out. I switched to Interior Design and stayed because I could erase mistakes with a pencil eraser.

I waited until the last minute to complete my work and struggled to maintain focus in the absence of stimulants such as coffee. I became easily interested in alcohol and recreational drugs, which made me feel more at ease. I was often nervous and embarrassed by things that came out of my mouth or the trouble I got into by interrupting people.

I used to work as an office designer and had difficulty keeping track of all my work and estimating accurate costs for parts because we had to count parts manually. This resulted in an excess of materials or a scarcity of parts. I counted and recounted several times and never got the same count twice.

As a young mother, the situation deteriorated. I discovered that I couldn't work while raising children because organising a household and caring for children was too much for me. I resigned and stayed at home with my children, but I was still a problem.

I was notorious for forgetting my children's piano lessons, dates with their friends, birthday parties, and soccer games. Because I didn't plan ahead of time, I mostly ended up at the store right before a party to pick up a gift and have it wrapped. I had no idea why I was this way and secretly despised myself. I worked very hard to improve.

I had to rush to school with supplies for items I had forgotten to send with my child, and I had to rely on friends to tell me when conferences or other parent involvement activities were taking place. I was constantly late picking up my children from school or activities, and I struggled with scheduling appointments, events, and running my home. I was completely irritated.

I was having marital problems and would frequently interrupt my husband when he was speaking. He spoke slowly and deliberately, and I would finish his sentences, which irritated him. Furthermore, the house was not clean, but rather cluttered and disorganised. I kept a lot of craft and art supplies around, but I never figured out how to organise or store them.

The stress of raising children and trying to keep up with everything we were doing was taxing on my already low self-esteem. My husband didn't think I was doing my fair share because I wasn't working and the house was always a mess.

What I did at the time to deal with all of this was to go to therapy.

- Attend marital therapy.
- I apologised profusely to my boss, husband, friends, and family.
- I postponed any organising until I had a full week or weekend.

- Continue to put off getting a job or returning to school.
- Pretend you've read more books than I have.
- Pretend to be more attentive than I am.
- Rely on friends for assistance, but make up excuses for why I need it.
- Read organising self-help books.
- Read self-help books on anything and everything.
- Enroll in a speed-reading class.
- Exercise
- Please accept my apologies for being late.
- Accept your apologies for forgetting things.
- Become depressed and attempt to disappear.
- Make no plans.
- Seek assistance from in-laws and family.
- I make plans, then cancel them when I realise I've double booked.

Finally, read Driven to Distraction, a book about ADHD.

I had many therapists for other co-occurring issues, but I inadvertently began living in a fantasy world, which led me to seek additional assistance.

The psychiatrist I saw asked me questions and listened to what I had to say for a while. It was the year 1999. Finally, he asked, "Have you ever considered that you might have ADHD?"

It took a long time to get the correct diagnosis and medications. My husband, on the other hand, noticed that I was paying attention to him and not interrupting him. His thoughts on the ADHD diagnosis and medications shifted. He was taken aback.

One aspect of ADHD that I appreciate is my creativity, which serves as a lifeline for me. Putting seemingly unrelated things together. I had this trait even before I started taking medications.

- I have a long list of issues that I struggle with, such as starting things and not finishing them.
- Messes and disorganisation abound because I leave them out to remind myself to return to it but then can't find what I need.
- Having a harder time remembering conversations or the names of artists and actors than others.
- I can't keep track of time.
- I can become overly focused on something unimportant and end up in stressful situations because I don't have time to do it right now.
- I frequently forget important tasks.
- Most of the time, I am late.
- On my phone, I have a zillion apps. I have too many calendars and to-do lists, but I lack the patience to deal with them.
- I'm not patient enough to delete documents.
- I lack the patience required to organise digital photos.
- I will NEVER find it if it is not organised.
- I have a habit of misplacing things.
- I'm on to the next thing before the first one is finished at work, and then I forget what I was doing and don't finish things.
- I don't have a steady job.

People usually agree when I tell them I have ADHD. They are, however, irritated if it occurs at work. I've told my friends, family, and children, as well as anyone else who needs to know. Many people find it amusing. Some people forget I have it and expect me to do things, then are surprised when I am late or forget. They don't understand that I try my hardest but still make mistakes. Most people do not believe it is as limiting as it appears to me.

After getting to know me, people realise I have ADHD. Still, I believe that people underestimate the impact on my mental health, self-esteem, time management, paper management, and so on, and may take things personally. As a result, they don't consider it when interpreting an interaction with me.

I enjoy being spontaneous, such as going for a late walk, stopping to admire nature, such as a sunset, riding a bike, walking, the breeze, nature in general, the lakefront, and good coffee. It's all very simple. On my iPhone, I enjoy drawing.

I'd say that the environment has been a primary passion of mine my entire life. I am also passionate about treating people with dignity and respect. I am passionate about assisting people with anxiety, ADHD, and their clutter issues and homes, but I have yet to act on that passion. I am passionate about art and design, photography, and food cultivation. I'm not involved in those areas. Most of the time, I just try not to lose too much money, stuff, or friends.

My friends and family both tell me that I'm far too hard on myself. They describe me as funny, compassionate, and intelligent, and they enjoy spending time with me. I want to believe those good things, but it's difficult for me. I need to break the habit of feeling bad about myself!

CHAPTER 4.

HOW TO DO PERFECT MEDITATION

You've now learned the fundamentals of meditation. You can keep practising these techniques at home. Daily meditation is beneficial to both the body and the mind, and it is something that anyone can do.

If you're ready to take the next step, joining a community meditation group or attending a retreat could be a great option.

Community meditation centres are frequently very encouraging and supportive of the meditative journey. It's a chance to meet like-minded people, pick up tips, and speak with members who are further along on their journey, or even assist brand new beginners in finding the right pose or meditation style. The centre may provide guided meditations, in which one person leads a group of people. This is not something you can accomplish at home when you are on your own. Sound meditations, such as gong therapy, also necessitate the presence of a second person. Is it also a good place to learn more advanced techniques like walking meditations or meditative yoga?

If there isn't anything like this nearby, you could form your own small meditation circle with a few friends, neighbours, and locals. To accomplish this, create a large space within your home by decluttering surrounding areas and covering distracting images or objects. Cushions should be scattered across the floor, preferably in a variety of colours. To enhance their experience, some attendees may wish to sit on a specific-colored cushion. Decide whether you'd prefer guided or individual silent meditation. If guided meditation is preferred, one person can lead the session, or a mindfulness CD can be played.

If you work long hours in an office, consider setting up a small room out of the way for you and your coworkers to have short meditation sessions at lunch. Your boss might be surprised at how much more productive your afternoons become.

A retreat is typically a longer and more concentrated way of experiencing the power of meditation. It can house a large number of members for a single day to several months.

Meditations will be scheduled throughout the day, from early morning to sunset, with no requirement to commit to a set number of sittings. Each retreat has its own set of rules, which should be read before making a reservation. Some may provide weekend packages or intensive full-day programmes. If you don't have any obligations at home, you might even prefer to devote a few weeks to progressing tremendously, both spiritually and physically.

A retreat is typically silent or very quiet, and it may also include workshops and opportunities to attend sessions with seasoned practitioners and monks. The room's silence is nurturing and wholesome, a welcome respite from a world full of televisions and cell phones.

Even meals are normally consumed mindfully, with full attention paid to the process of tasting and swallowing, flavours and colours.

If you want to try something new with your meditation practise, bring a blanket and a cushion to a large outdoor area away from crowds and try an outdoor session. This will be very different from your home environment, with new and unusual sounds, smells, and sensations. Practice mindfulness by becoming aware of how the wind feels on your cheeks, how the birds sing to one another, how the flowers smell, and how the grass feels beneath your legs.

Is there a difference in the way the air feels when you breathe it in? Is it getting colder? Fresher?

Finally, begin to hone the skill of meditating anywhere. Begin small, such as with a park bench in a dog walking area, so that passersby are present but not disruptive. The beach is a wonderful sensory experience that also tests one's concentration. Remember that meditating isn't about buying tools and instruments or needing 'things,' it's about something you have inside of you—an ability—that you can use and enjoy at any time and from anywhere.

Simple Meditation Techniques

Meditation comes in a variety of styles and forms. These types have essentially come from various religions, cultures, or countries around the world. The following are the most well-known types of meditation:

- Buddhism meditation based on religion.
- Yoga and Hinduism (Dhyana).
- Islam (Sufi).
- Christian contemplation.
- Jain meditative practise.

Each of the aforementioned meditation types has distinct representations and methods of meditation. However, the purpose of this book is to explain simple methods of meditation that any modern person can do at home, office, park, etc., and it is an extract of all meditation types that tries to explain.

Meditation Preparation

Let me highlight some key points for meditation preparation:

- Choose a quiet, clean location. If you prefer, you can use an earplug to block out outside noise.
- "Focus Object:" Choose any focal point. It could be your breath, a burning candle, a vision board, a mantra, or something else.
- Make sure you have a comfortable mat or chair.
- Wear something comfortable.
- Maintain a straight spine while sitting. It's not too tight, but it's a comfortable fit. It serves two functions. First and

83

foremost, it will keep you awake. Second, blood circulation is excellent in this position.

- Your position should be alert and relaxing. Only one of them will be unsuitable for a good position.
- The best time to meditate is in the morning or before going to bed. However, if you choose either one or both, keep it consistent.
- Eat no more than an hour before meditation.

Some Crucial Mental Preparation

I don't believe I have to work hard to concentrate or focus during meditation. That is not the case. Meditation is simple, but it requires perseverance. Feel your true self and the outside world without judgement.

- Expect no miracles or immediate results. Don't expect any specific results during or after meditation. The desire to pay attention can sometimes be an impediment to concentration. So don't wish for anything and don't expect anything. However, enjoy the journey, the peace, calm, and relaxation, and feel love for yourself and the outside world.
- Take advantage of the time you have to yourself.
- Don't be concerned if a distraction appears. Just ignore that distraction/sound and keep going.
- The key to meditation is to effortlessly return to your "object of focus" when your mind wanders. And being persistent entails doing this on a daily basis.

Meditation Techniques

In today's world, there are essentially two types of meditation.

- Meditation with a focus.
- Mindfulness is a popular term for awareness-based meditation.

Meditation with Concentration

1. The timer can also be set for 5/10/15 minutes to ensure that you know when to start and when to stop. If you want, your habit will gradually eliminate the need for time.

2. Attempt to concentrate on your "object of focus" with ease.

Close your eyes and concentrate on your breath, a candle, or whatever object you prefer. Be natural and free of stress (remember, no results are expected). You've started meditating now.

3. Assume you are concentrating on your breathing. After 3 or 4 breaths, your mind will begin to wander. And you'll notice it after 5–10 seconds. This time is determined by your emotional attachment to the subject matter and where your mind is going. If you have recently experienced job stress, you may spend more time thinking about it. In most cases, it takes 5–10 seconds. When under stress, one requires more time to meditate than usual. There's an old adage about meditation that goes, "Half an hour of meditation every day is essential, except when you're busy." Then an hour is required." In any case, recognising that you were thinking about something else and not focusing on your "object of focus" for a few seconds is a significant milestone in your meditation

practise. This realisation is said to be the result of meditation. Because this is the point at which you are no longer attached to your mind's thoughts (good or bad), and you are yourself, and you now have the ability to control your attention.

4. Now that you've regained control of yourself, you can effortlessly/naturally/willingly shift your attention back to your "object of focus." Consider your focus on your "inner eyes."

Just as you can shift your focus from an object you don't want to see to one you do, you can shift your inner focus (attention) from your thoughts to your breath (object of focus). Try to concentrate on your "object of focus" for as long as you can. Not forcefully, but with determination. Re-adjust your focus whenever you are distracted by thoughts. You may eventually find yourself at peace and at the centre of the universe. You may have the impression that your "self" (ego) is dissolving and that you are a part of a larger universe. You will be more aware or alert, and you will feel more confident that you are in control of your life. These are the outcomes of my meditations. The most important aspect of meditation is to feel calm and peaceful while doing it.

5. During a single meditation session, you will go into thoughts and return to your object of focus several times. Don't give up and enjoy the peace and quiet. After some practise, perhaps a couple of months, you will notice that your control and ability to concentrate on an object has improved. You are no longer easily distracted by what is going on around you. This concentration power will be very useful in your work and in your life in general, as it will increase your productivity. What's more, you will.

6. Don't judge yourself during the concentration practise based on how well or poorly you are doing. Because of stress from outside work or excitement about good things coming into your life or work, your mind will wander more on some days than others.

You may have negative feelings about meditation at times. It's not working, it's boring, it's frustrating, and it's not helping me. However, these are the feelings that everyone has when they begin meditating. You will find it difficult to concentrate in these situations. But leave it alone. Don't push yourself any further. But the key is that you willingly drag your attention back when your mind wanders. Perseverance is the key to successful focus-based meditation.

7. After a few months of good concentration practise, one's ability to focus on one thing develops, and one can easily distinguish between its one of focus and its random thought (by which one gets distracted during meditation).

This awareness of distinguishing between your "object of focus" and "your thoughts" (good/bad/random) rather than becoming engrossed in these thoughts, aids in the transition to awareness-based meditation or mindfulness meditation. As a result, it is best to start with focus-based meditation before moving on to mindfulness meditation.

Meditation Based on Awareness (Mindfulness)

During focus-based meditation, we concentrate on the "object of focus" and maintain constant contact with it. We are aware of the object.

In mindfulness meditation, however, we simply feel present, becoming aware of the truth of the present. Moment by moment, we become aware of what is already true. You are aware of your surroundings or your inner world, or even your breath "object of focus," but you no longer focus on it constantly. You free your mind and experience the joy of the present moment. Most people are not aware of their surroundings at any given time.

Their thoughts are consumed by their worries, plans, regrets, fears, and so on. They are either living in the past or in the future. It's okay to plan for the future or analyse the past from time to time, but constant worrying is bad and sucks when people's minds are elsewhere than their bodies. This is unnatural and destroys everything within us.

Mindfulness is the polar opposite of this. Mindfulness allows you to live in the present moment, with your body and your surroundings, and peace, positivity, and happiness flow naturally. Consider children, who are always in the present moment and are more joyful and energetic than adults.

We simply observe reality as it is in mindfulness meditation. You simply observe your thoughts as they arise and then pass away/disappear after a few seconds, without passing any judgement. You will soon become aware of the constant arising and passing of thought as constant flux. And you'll realise that this constant thought flow is unimportant and draining your mental energy. This is due to the fact that your thoughts are constantly changing. You will eventually realise that it is not necessary to be absorbed by every thought and feeling.

Your ego will eventually melt, and you will melt. This is the real deal when it comes to mindfulness meditation. It is important to note that mindfulness meditation is not about "NOT THINKING." Thought will follow. It's enough to notice them without passing judgement; don't try to get rid of them.

Meditation Methods

Visualization

During our discussion of stillness, we briefly mentioned visualisation. Visualization is a tool that I enjoy using, particularly with my Fruits of the Spirit meditations. You can use this to help you meditate by stilling and relaxing your mind and spirit. You see, it's a literal representation of something that can represent what you're meditating on.

It serves as both an allegory for your meditation and something to enjoy. Assume you're meditating on peace. What kind of peaceful image could you conjure up in your mind? Perhaps it's a lovely waterfall or lake. Take your time visualising the image and framing it within the quality you're meditating on.

A beautiful, majestic tree could be a perfect visualisation to still the mind and body and focus on when using the Fruits of the Spirit. This tree could be a massive fruit tree in an orchard or a forest, blooming with delectable fruit on every branch. That fruit represents the fruit you're growing within yourself. You could be practising kindness; this is a kindness tree with kindness fruit. What is your favourite type of tree fruit? Perhaps that will conjure up images of kindness for you. It could be a peach tree in bloom. If you're meditating on a few fruits, imagine yourself in an orchard with various types of fruit trees, each representing a different fruit. Don't be concerned about whether or not this fruit will grow in the same climate as that fruit. It's a representation of heaven within you.

Visualization can also be used to see yourself doing or accomplishing something. If you meditate on patience, you may see yourself being more patient in a situation and how those around you are happier and blessed as a result of your increased patience. You can see anything that is not of high quality fading away. See that anger leaving you if you aren't a gentle person because of it.

You might see it as a cloud leaving you. That is one way to employ visualisation.

When visualising, you don't always have to use a specific quality. If I'm listening to music with environmental sounds, I'll sometimes visualise what I'm hearing, which can be quite calming and peaceful in and of itself. If you want, you can link it to your larger meditation. I may even see someone playing an instrument or a musical note for the music on occasion. You might be hearing a violin and picturing yourself playing it.

As you can see, there are a plethora of ways to incorporate visualisation into meditation. As you concentrate on the fruit's meditation, you can combine it with the other techniques listed below. If you don't want to, don't feel obligated to visualise throughout the meditation. During a 45-minute meditation session, I probably only visualise for a few minutes at most. I just know it's always there for me.

Affirmation

We've looked at the power of affirmations in a relaxed state to reprogram your mind for more positive beliefs and perspectives on the world around you. Affirmations can change your state of mind and give you the confidence to do almost anything. Affirmations can help you reduce and eventually eliminate negative beliefs and emotions about yourself. If you say them enough times, you will believe them, even if you don't completely believe them at first. I had mentioned that I struggled with feelings of being a loser. "I'm a winner," is one affirmation I've been using. I rarely feel like a loser anymore, and instead believe that I am a winner who can achieve anything I set my mind to.

What always goes hand in hand with your affirmations is to push yourself a little bit each day, getting out of your comfort zone.

Affirmations with fruits can take many different forms. You can affirm that you feel peace, that you have peace, that you are at peace, and so on.

You can affirm those you love, such as "I love my kids," "I love my spouse," and "I love myself." You can also affirm that you are loved by those in your life. As long as it's positive, you can be creative by affirming the fruits. One area where you might try to push yourself with the fruits is patience. Declare that you are patient, and then look for opportunities to practise patience in your daily life. It will not be difficult to find opportunities to practise patience if you have children. Kids have a habit of bringing them up all the time!

When it comes to meditation, I've never been a fan of mantras. To some extent, however, I have also used the fruits as a kind of mantra at times.

I don't always want to say full phrase affirmations when I'm deeply relaxed, so I'll just say "love," "joy," or "peace" over and over for a while. Sometimes I'll do "love and peace" combinations. Try to feel the emotion or quality within yourself when you do mantras or single-word affirmations. Feel what love, peace, or gentleness are.

Gratitude

Gratefulness is a vital practise that can transform your life and the way you perceive everything around you. The fruits represent an opportunity to practise gratitude in your meditation. You can express gratitude for the fruits of love, peace, and joy. You can be thankful for the times in your life when you felt such qualities and expressed them.

When was the last time you felt or showed love? Take the time to reflect on and be grateful for those moments in meditation. Do the same with all of the fruits. Even fruits that appear difficult or less "fun," such as patience or self-control, can be beneficial.

Be thankful for the opportunities to demonstrate the fruits you've had and will have as you meditate on them every day. Consider yourself to be growing in the fruits. View your progress from where you are to where you were. Consider the areas where you can still grow and be thankful that you have the opportunity to make meaningful changes right now.

Finally, be thankful for the positive feelings that come from being more loving, peaceful, joyful, patient, kind, good, faithful, gentle, and self-controlled. It can be a wonderful euphoric feeling to experience and express your life's fruits.

Reflections

Take some time during your meditation to reflect on what each fruit means to you in your life. You can use mindfulness, affirmations, gratitude, and visualisation, or you can simply reflect. You might consider where I am in terms of kindness, where I need to improve, and how I can be more kind.

When was the last time I showed kindness or someone else showed kindness to me, and it really touched me? This is something you can do with any fruit.

Reflection probably consumes the majority of my meditation time these days. I frequently combine it with other techniques, such as affirmations. Reflection is an important component of most religions, and it is what meditation is used for to a large extent. When the Bible mentions meditation, it frequently refers to taking time to reflect.

It is also central to meditation in Buddhism. Meditation reflection is a method of self-examination of one's life. Examining your life through the fruits is an excellent way to develop emotionally and spiritually.

How do I begin to think about meditation and my life in general? One simple method is to use what I refer to as the questions. Who is it, when is it, where is it, why is it, and how is it done? In relation to the fruits, ask them about yourself and your life.

93

CHAPTER 5.

16 RELAXING FAIRY TALES

Bentley Hippo's Adventures: Inspiring Children to Be Patient Dedication

This story is dedicated to anyone who is unable to sit still. Being patient is difficult, but it is critical. It is not always easy to do the right thing.

'Patience' is a virtue.

- Reduces the likelihood of worrying about things.
- It benefits both your physical and mental health.
- It is a way to practise kindness while also making you feel good.

Let's go on this adventure with Bentley as he teaches Jaxon, our little monkey with ADHD, how to be patient.

It was early morning. A loud knock came at the front door. Bentley noticed Jaxon pacing back and forth through the peephole.

Bentley pushed open the door. Jaxon was so enthralled that he couldn't speak clearly. All Bentley could make out were the words 'ride,' 'hurry,' and 'long lineup.'

Bentley shook his head, deciding it was easier to go see what all the fuss was about than to try to get Jaxon to repeat his words. They followed the big arrows down a long path and into an open field.

It was extremely crowded, with people walking around eating ice cream, a variety of noises, and long lines. They made their way to the open field.

There was a long line, and Bentley noticed Daisy the Giraffe, Toby the Elephant, and Marty the Lion near the back.

"What's going on?" Bentley inquired. "There was an announcement—the blue rocket will be lifting off today only, and it is supposed to be the ride of a lifetime," Marty explained. Jaxon's pupils dilated. "That's what I was saying earlier," he told Bentley.

Bentley paused for a moment. Hmmm, a once-in-a-lifetime ride? This must be the reason for the long line of children; and where did they get the ice cream cones? Bentley, Jaxon, and Daisy waited in line while Marty and Toby went to get ice cream cones for everyone.

They came back and joined the others. After a few minutes, Jaxon became irritated. He dashed to the front of the line and attempted to slip in. He was returned. He couldn't stop moving. He tried again and was again relegated to the back.

95

He became frustrated as he jumped up and down, trying to catch a glimpse of the front. He stomped harder and louder with each jump.

The ground shook so violently at one point that everyone's ice cream fell to the ground. Jaxon was too frustrated to notice the sad faces staring at him. He was still attempting to find a way to the front.

Bentley was irritated by Jaxon's behaviour and the fact that he had misplaced his ice cream. Taking away his ice cream is the one thing that can make a happy hippo unhappy! "I'm overjoyed!" "Bentley, Bentley, stop frowning!" exclaimed Jaxon. It's going to be a lot of fun!"

"Stop!" Bentley exclaimed. "Just be still! But I'm ecstatic!" Jaxon \sargued. "We're all excited, but we're not jumping around and trying to push in!"

Just then, the ticket agent approached and warned them that if they didn't calm down, they wouldn't be allowed on the ride. Jaxon let out a long sigh, and the ticket agent made his way back to the front. Bentley was aware that Jaxon occasionally became overly excited and struggled to remain still, and that his actions were not deliberate. Bentley, on the other hand, didn't want to miss out on the trip. He took a deep breath; he would have to practise patience as well.

"It's unfair to try to jump ahead of the line, Jaxon," Bentley began to explain. "I understand," he said. "And your bouncing up and down had an effect on those around you." Then you started arguing, which is unacceptable, especially since you know how important it is to be kind to others. You must be patient."

Bentley could tell Jaxon was sorry, but he wasn't sure what it meant to be patient. When you're patient, you have to keep your

96

cool even when you're excited. There are things you can do to help if you are feeling impatient. You enjoy directing your attention to others and conversing with them!

You could also play a game like 'I spy,' take deep breaths or try this: Examine the clouds. Can you tell what the shapes are? Everyone looked up and described the shapes they saw in the clouds. "Triangle! Circle! Bunny!"

Bentley told everyone how much he loved space, and they were at the front of the line before they knew it!

"I see you all did exactly what I asked," said the ticket agent.

The agent handed them tickets after Jaxon quickly nodded.

With huge grins on their faces, they looked at their tickets, then at each other, then back at the tickets. "Follow me," the agent said. They were escorted around the bend. It was right there. The massive blue rocket. It wasn't, however, a rocket. They were perplexed. "Where has the blue rocket gone?" Jaxon inquired.

Bentley's friends looked at him, knowing he must be disappointed because this didn't appear to be the trip to the moon. It was a massive hot-air balloon.

Bentley shrugged, looked at Marty, then at Jaxon, and said, "Well, it's not a rocket ship, but it's really cool." Let's hop on and take a ride."

Jaxon took a step forward, looked around, and asked, "Who wants to get on first?" When everyone was aboard, the balloon took off, flying high into the sky. Everyone had a great time. They looked down at the children below, who appeared to be tiny dots.

"This ride is incredible," Toby exclaimed. Bentley smiled at his companions. This isn't what I expected, but Jaxon learned about patience today, and if he hadn't knocked on my door, we would never have gotten this far.

It's the highest I've ever been and the closest I've ever come to space, and I'm glad you're all here with me. They looked at Jaxon, who was in his own world, reaching out and grabbing some clouds. Everyone laughed, including Jaxon.

Bentley taught yet another wonderful and important lesson. There are numerous activities you can engage in to improve your patience. Here are a few examples; see if you can think of any more.

- Draw or colour a picture.
- You can play with your toys or with your friends.
- Make jokes.
- Make a list of everything for which you are grateful.
- You should read a book.

Ellie, the ADHD Super Heroine

Pssst. Do you hear what I'm saying? Do you notice me? No? Take a closer look!

See? I'm quite small, but I'm here.

Hello there! I'm here! My name is Fay, and I'm Ellie's little helper. I'd like to introduce you to a person. Where have you gone, Ellie?

You've arrived. This is Ellie, by the way. She is a four-year-old girl, and I assist her with a variety of tasks. How can I assist her? I'll explain.

When Ellie sits down for breakfast every morning, I whisper in her ear, " "It's good for you, Ilie, to eat a slice of bread, especially

98

this whole wheat bread that Mommy buys, with cucumber slices and a tasty hard-boiled egg. Isn't it delectable?" As a result, Ellie eats a nutritious breakfast every day. She is always prepared for the day ahead of her.

When Ellie is struggling to sit still while her teacher reads a story in kindergarten, I whisper in her ear, "Let's go outside and play" (of course with the teacher's assistant).

Ellie jumps and rages outside in the open air, climbs the slide, and swings on the swing. "Come on Ellie, let's go back," I say, and Ellie walks back into the kindergarten, sits quietly, and listens to the end of the story with the other kids.

I occasionally assist Ellie's parents. If Ellie has completed a beautiful painting, cleaned up all of her toys, or assisted Mommy in setting the table for dinner, I whisper in their ears, "Give Ellie praise for all of her creations and for every chore she completes." Ellie feels safe and loved when they tell her how much they appreciate her paintings and assistance. Don't you like it when you're appreciated?

I also request that they inform Ellie to set the table every evening. This is a vital job because they wouldn't be able to eat anything without her, isn't it, kid?

Ellie's parents agreed to send her to gymnastics three times a week after school because I requested it. I know it helps Ellie focus, stay disciplined, and set and achieve her own goals. (Doing what you enjoy can also be beneficial.) "Feed Ellie healthy food," I say into her parents' ears. When they go shopping, they buy a lot of fruits and vegetables, as well as salmon, which is very good for her and makes her feel more relaxed and happy.

When Ellie is in a bad mood and jumping around the house in the afternoon, I whisper in her ear, "Let's race each other on the grass outside. If you can, catch me!" Ellie feels a lot better after we go outside with Mommy and Daddy.

"Make a dream board, so you can see what to do next," I say in Ellie's ear whenever she is sad or feels she isn't good at anything.

As a result, her Mommy and Daddy assist her in putting numerous pictures on the board.

She receives a special treat or a star whenever she completes a task on the board. You can also make a dream board if you want! Ellie has a unique talent—she is extremely musical. She enjoys playing her father's guitar and listening intently to every beautiful melody she hears.

Her mother is constantly watching her play. "Is Ellie really talented, Mommy?" I ask in her ear. Tell her if that's the case."

Before bedtime, I recommend Ellie drink a glass of fresh orange juice squeezed by her father. When she's finished, we both fall asleep quickly and dream until the next morning. I am overjoyed to tell you about Ellie and all the ways I assist her on a daily basis. I'm sure you have your own little assistant deep within you who whispers in your ear and tells you what the best thing to do next, right?

Who Is a Pretty Boy, Ian, My Autistic Friend?

Paco, my name is Paco, and I'm a talking parrot. How did I learn to speak? I lived with the Bells for a few years. Mr. Travis, the father, loved to teach me all kinds of tricks, including how to talk. The Peterson family paid us a visit on Sunday. That's when I first met Ian, their son.

I'm used to children, but their requests drive me insane: "Paco says hello! Paco is counting to ten! "Paco, what's your name?"

Ian, on the other hand. Ian didn't say anything. He maintained his distance from me. I believe my voice bothered him, and he would occasionally sneak a peek at me. I couldn't figure it out. I was even slightly offended.

Why was Ian behaving so differently than the rest of the group? I was afraid he didn't like me at all.

The Petersons had left, and I had returned to my normal routine. But the following Sunday, Ian and his mother paid us another visit. I wondered why he was here again if he didn't want to be my friend.

Oh, I forgot to mention that last week, in between the two visits, Mr. Travis taught me to say aloud, "Ian, Ian," in the hopes that if I saw him again, he would like me more. "Ian, Ian," I said, and Ian turned to face me. Another week has passed, and guess who showed up on Sunday?

Ian, you are correct. "Ian, Ian," I called, and Ian came closer and smiled at the same time.

The following week, Ian sat down next to me, and whenever I called out, "Ian, Ian," he repeated after me, "Ian."

I was looking forward to Sunday the following week. And Ian, I felt he already liked me, so I showed off a little and called "one, two, three," which Ian repeated after me.

Ian's mother was overjoyed. She burst out laughing, and I couldn't help but smile because, according to Ian's mother, Ian had never spoken before. So the Bells asked me a very important question because I'm so helpful to Ian and Ian adores me, and I immediately agreed, "Yes, yes," I said.

In Ian's house, I moved into a fancy cage. We would spend every available moment together after that day. Ian would make sure I had water and food, and he'd even pet me a little.

I taught Ian to call me "Paco, Paco" and to count to ten. "How are you doing?" "How are you?" I'd ask Ian every morning, and he'd respond, "How are you?"

"Paco, today we're going to visit Ian's kindergarten," Ian's mother told me one morning. Oh, no! I hid my face in my wings. Who has so many children's patience? But that morning, my heart melted as I saw Ian proudly introducing me to all the kindergarten students and asking, "Paco, will you say hello?" Can you count to ten, Paco? "Paco, what's your name?" On that day, Ian was king of the kindergarten for the first time, and I walked around between the kids, swelling with pride and feeling so proud of my friend, Ian.

Ellie, the ADHD Supergirl, Wins First Grade

How are things going for you? Remember how we met before? You were in kindergarten at the time. You've come a long way since then. Hello, my name is Fay. Ellie's personal assistant. Do you recall Ellie? No? Ellie is the ADD/ADHD Supergirl.

Ellie has also grown. She is now in first grade, just like you. But sitting in a classroom for so many hours and listening to the teacher isn't easy, is it? So I'm here to assist. I assist Ellie, the teacher, and possibly you as well. Do you want to know how I did it?

"Ellie, let's play a little with the sandbox at the edge of the classroom," I say in Ellie's ear as she starts moving impatiently in her chair. Helen, the teacher, approves.

We approach the kinetic sandbox quietly. We knead and combine it.

Mountains and ravines are formed by us. We make a few miniature cakes. Not for long, only a few minutes.

I occasionally remind Ellie, "You have bicycle pedals under your desk, Ellie. Make use of them! It will help you focus and pay attention to Teacher Helen." "

During the breaks between classes, we rush to the sensory path. Is there a path like this at your school? It's a fantastic activity that allows Ellie to burn off some energy while also studying.

What can you do in it, you may wonder? You can jump in any shape you want.

You can walk down the lines, play hopscotch, or simply take a break. You can relax by taking a deep breath.

We enjoy competing with one another. Which of us will be the first to complete the entire track?

Sometimes I whisper in Teacher Helen's ear that if she gives Ellie stars for completing chores, it will encourage Ellie to work hard and earn more and more stars. Do you get stars as well?

For what purpose?

When Ellie appears unsettled in class, I have a magical solution for her: Theraplast! What exactly is it, you ask? It's putty, but it doesn't stink and doesn't make a mess. Ellie kneads it, stretches it all over the place, and rolls it into a ball. It aids Ellie in holding her pencil correctly. Ellie is more focused when she uses it?

When Ellie is having difficulty sitting in her chair, I tell her, "Let's go read our book on the beanbags at the edge of the classroom."

We get up quietly, walk over to the beanbags, and relax.

Ellie works best when Teacher Helen gives her simple and clear instructions and writes them on the board in an orderly fashion, in numbered lists that begin with 1, 2, and 3. Is it the same with your teacher?

Do you know what else makes Ellie's classroom unique? That each child handles something at which he or she excels. Ellie, for example, is in charge of quickly erasing the board at the end of each lesson and ensuring that Teacher Helen has enough markers in each colour for the next lesson. That's a huge responsibility, isn't it?

During breaks, when we aren't on the sensory path, we eat something from Ellie's mom's lunch box, which she prepares for us every morning. Mommy makes us small sandwiches with wholewheat bread, sliced vegetables, and fruit. Yummy! What kind of food do you eat at school?

Remember how I told you Ellie is an excellent gymnast?

Ellie is asked to demonstrate an exercise in front of the entire class once a week by Teacher Helen. Every child in the class shows his classmates something he excels at once a week. Isn't that a brilliant idea? What are your strong points?

Every day, an entire lesson is dedicated to working with apps on a tablet. Ellie is enthralled by this lesson. She is perfectly content to sit quietly for nearly an hour and practise reading, writing, and math. It's a fantastic way to study, in my opinion.

Do you have any idea what else Teacher Helen does? Occasionally, during class, she will tell everyone to stop working, get up, and stand by their chair. Then she leads us in stretching our hands up, shaking our legs slightly, jumping in place, and sitting back in our chairs, more focused and ready to learn. Isn't Helen a fantastic teacher?

Oh, I almost forgot to mention another fun item that helps Ellie concentrate: a balance pad! Do you have any idea what it is? There is a special pad on the floor at the edge of the classroom, next to the wall.

Any child who is sick of sitting can approach the pad, stand on it, stabilise himself, and try not to fall off.

What are we going to do when we get home from school? First, we take Ellie's mother and father to a nearby park and play on the grass.

Then I assist Ellie with her homework. Teacher Helen understands how difficult it is for Ellie to focus for an extended period of time, so she assigns Ellie very little homework so that she can exercise a little on her own and succeed like everyone else. Is that how it is with you as well?

Ellie's mother reads us a short story before we go to bed.

We fall asleep quickly under the dim light of the starlight lamp and sleep soundly until the next morning. Good night to you as well, kid.

Speaking Without Using Words

I vividly recall sitting alone on a beach near the still waters. Everything was calm and quiet, and I was as well.

The ocean became very tumultuous all of a sudden, and a deafening noise surrounded me. I shut my eyes and covered both of my ears with my hands. When I opened my eyes again, there was a strange creature standing in the sea in front of me. It was unlike anything I'd ever experienced. I was terrified. I was terrified and looked for cover, but there was none. There was only me and the strange creature.

Who was it that waved at me with his "hands" like this?

I closed my eyes again, this time tightly. Maybe the strange creature will flee? But he was still standing there, signalling to me with his "hands" like this. I made the decision to be brave. I raised my hand and waved to the strange creature in this manner, and he waved back.

We got closer one step at a time. When he got to the beach, the strange creature bent down and drew my image in the soft sand with his long finger, then waved his hands like this.

I thought I understood what he was saying, so I said aloud, "My name is Dean." Perhaps he had realised? Then he clapped his hands and pointed to himself before pointing to the sea, as if to say, "That's where I'm from."

I knelt and drew a smiley face in the sand, and he smiled a strange creature's smile. So we sat on the sand, face to face, and drew: I drew a sandwich, he drew a fish. He drew seaweed, while I drew a banana. I drew myself playing computer games, while he drew himself riding a whale. I drew myself reading a book, while he drew himself catching a lobster.

After a while, I and the strange creature were completely acquainted.

We became really good friends through our drawings, without using our voices or words. As the sun began to set, it was time to return home. My strange creature friend waved goodbye and returned to the sea. I was a little disappointed, but I was glad we had met. So, thank you strange creature, I now know how to make friends with other creatures as well!

Who is Jordan?

Jordan is my name. He's only five years old. He is the son of a father and a mother, and he has an older brother, a younger sister, and a dog named Buddy. Jordan can count to ten and recognises all of the colours. He can build things out of blocks and draw amazing pictures.

He enjoys reading and can already recognise a few letters. He knows the names of all the birds and flowers in the garden. Jordan, on the other hand, has no friends! Jordan goes to kindergarten every morning and plays dice, puzzles, and outside in the yard by himself. And when he goes on trips, he walks alone in the back.

"Perhaps I'll wear my best clothes today and then I'll have friends," Jordan reasoned one morning.

As a result, Jordan dressed up for kindergarten. Jordan was startled to hear, "Psst! Psst!" "Who is that?" he wondered to himself. "Who is it that's calling?"

Jordan looked in every direction, but he couldn't find anyone speaking to him. "Sssst! Ssst!" — "I'm here, under the table," Jordan heard the voice say again. Jordan knelt down and peered beneath the table, but he saw nothing and no one. "Over here, Jordan, I'm here," the voice said again.

When he looked closely, he noticed a green, slimy, fat, and ugly caterpillar crawling on one of the table's legs.

"Yuck," Jordan exclaimed. "What a nasty caterpillar," he exclaimed.

"Jordan, come here; I have something to tell you." The caterpillar murmured from the table's bottom. Jordan took a seat beneath the table, next to the caterpillar. "Pleased to meet you; my name is Larry, and I'd like to tell you a secret," the caterpillar continued.

"Even without your best clothes, I think you're a handsome, smart, and talented young man." Jordan told himself the next day, "Maybe today I'll wear a cool cap and then I'll have friends."

"Sssst! Ssst!" From beneath the table, Jordan heard Larry the caterpillar's familiar voice. "Jordan, this cool hat is only for show. "Prove to everyone that you're smart, knowledgeable, and a good friend."

Jordan told himself, "I'll get a haircut." "I'll go to the barbershop and get a cool hairstyle, and then I'll have friends."

"Jordan, get a haircut." "That's always a good idea," Larry said quietly from beneath the table, "but don't you understand? With or without a haircut, you're always cool and successful. I'll ask Dad for his old phone and show it off to all the kindergarten kids, and then I'll have friends." "Jordan," Larry lamented, "how many times do I have to tell you?"

You're a wonderful kid, phone or no phone, and anyone who isn't your friend is missing out. Larry the caterpillar vanished one morning! Jordan was starting to like him and their conversations under the table, despite the fact that he wasn't particularly attractive.

Jordan searched every table corner for Larry, whispering his name over and over, but received no response. All he found was an obscure grey lump marking the spot where he first met Larry.

Larry did not return after a few days. Jordan, on the other hand, remembered all of his conversations with Larry, and because he was now certain that he was the best in the world, he made more and more friends.

Jordan was playing dice with his kindergarten friends when he heard a familiar, friendly voice say, "Psst! Psst!" Jordan."

Jordan dove under the table right away, calling out, "Larry, where are you?" but he didn't see a green, slimy, fat, and ugly caterpillar under the table. All he saw in front of him was a large, elegant butterfly with gracefully flapping wings.

"Hello, Jordan—my name is Larry. You used to think I was disgusting and ugly; how do you feel about me now? "You're the same, Jordan," Larry said as he finished his victory speech. "Like me, you are beautiful on the inside, smart, and talented, and one day you will spread your wings and everyone will see your beauty," he said as he flew away—Jordan no longer needed him.

Since then, whenever Jordan thinks he has no friends because he isn't good enough looking, smart enough, or likeable, he recalls his friend Larry the caterpillar/butterfly, and his face lights up with a huge smile as he runs to join the game at the table.

- The Life Cycle of a Butterfly
- A mother butterfly lays a large number of eggs on a plant.
- When an egg hatches, a caterpillar eats the plant leaves.
- The caterpillar then sheds its skin and emerges as a cocoon.

109

- When it's ready, a lovely butterfly emerges from its cocoon.
- The mother butterfly lays her eggs once more, and the cycle continues.

Can You See Who I Am?

Hello, my name is Emma, and I'd like to tell you about my kindergarten friends.

We all go to kindergarten every morning. We all have a good time at kindergarten once everyone has arrived. Playing with dice, singing, and dancing, frolicking in the yard, and going for walks on occasion.

Sarah, our teacher, asked us that morning, 'What makes you unique?' Every day, we all do the same thing, I thought— sometimes I feel like we're all the same! But as I walked around the playground, I realised how unique we all are.

Mia is cheerful and giddy all day. Sarah, the teacher, is amused as well.

Everyone is happy and laughing when she is around. Ben always helps everyone: he helps Jayden say goodbye to Mom, he assists Mason in caring for the animals, he assists teacher Sarah in gathering all the children, and he even assists in repairing the dripping tap in the sink.

Emily is inquisitive; she is constantly asking questions such as, "How do you make clothes?" How many different colours are there in the world? Is there life in space?

Liam is well-versed in everything. He's the first to respond to any question posed by the kindergarten teacher; he knows the date, the colour of the sky, and the names of all the flowers in the garden. He even recognises a few letters.

Aria is a wonderful friend to all. She always smiles when she sees me, Mia, Ben, Emily, Liam, and Mason—everyone! Mason is a huge animal lover. He makes friends with every cat that passes through the backyard and assists beetles in overcoming obstacles. He even looks after the ants, making sure no one enters their nest.

Lily is a natural athlete, jumping and hopping all day, dangling from the monkey bars in the yard and doing cartwheels in the air.

Jayden has a lot of goals. He aspires to be an astronaut when he grows up.

Kaylee is constantly drawing, pasting various leaves on paper, and constructing beautiful houses out of cubes. She has a lot of imagination. Dylan is a fantastic actor, spending the entire day doing impressions of Mom and Dad, as well as teacher Sarah. He can even imitate the sounds of a dog, cat, parrot, and crow. He can imitate any sound you ask him to.

Leah is extremely generous. She is always eager to include others in games, to share her sandwich and apple, and even her new drawing chalks with the other children. Jaxon never gets angry and always forgives anyone who pushes him, refuses to play with him, or speaks ill of him. Jaxon is never bitter. Elena adores everyone, constantly hugging the other children, teacher Sarah, and even Wally the kindergarten's pet turtle. Logan is our leader, always announcing what needs to be done and directing us to play in the yard or take a quick nap together.

Camila is always neat and clean. She doesn't get dirty even when we're colouring with paint. She always puts each book in its proper place and collects all of the toys.

David excels at the piano in kindergarten. I enjoy listening to his music because it is so beautiful. Teacher Sarah informed us that David is autistic—I didn't really understand it, or I didn't care because I love him so much. And what about me? I know how to tell fantastic stories!

So I realised that each of us is unique and special, with our own little treasures hidden within us. What about you? What distinguishes you? What treasure do you have within you?

Dana, too, deserves a playground.

There is so much to do on the playground! Swings, merrygo-rounds, climbing nets, and slides are available. There are a lot of kids at the playground: small kids, big kids, and kids of all colours.

They bring their fathers or mothers, grandfathers or grandmothers, as well as all of their friends. The kids swing on the swings, slide down the slides, and climb on the climbers. They are all happy, laughing, and having a good time.

Dana visits the playground with her father on a regular basis, but she is unable to run and jump, climb and slide, or swing on the swings. This is due to Dana's use of a wheelchair. She looks around at the other kids, sad. She wished she could swing on the swings, spin on the carousel, and play like the other kids. Daniel, a young boy, noticed Dana sitting alone. "Why aren't you playing?" Daniel inquired. "I can't," Dana replied. "I'm in a wheelchair, and there's nothing I can do here." Daniel dashed over to his mother.

"Dana isn't allowed to play on the playground, Mom!" Dana is confined to a wheelchair!

"How can we assist her?" Another youngster, Jonathan, tugged at his grandmother's sleeve. "Something must be done!

Dana is confined to a wheelchair, but she should be able to swing, spin, and play. "What else can we do?"

"Dad, Dad!" exclaimed Leah as she dashed up to her father—"Dana's in a wheelchair! "How can we make a swing that works for her, as well as a slide or a merry-go-round?"

Dana did not go to the playground the next day, nor the day after that. Dana did not return to the playground after many days. Daniel, Jonathan, and Leah gathered all of the other kids in the playground, as well as their parents and grandparents. They brainstormed, and brainstormed, and brainstormed some more equipment for Dana to play with.

They sat together for an entire day, then another, and another.

Many more days passed before they figured it out! They enlisted the help of engineers, surveyors, carpenters, and metalworkers, all of whom worked and worked and worked—until they were finally finished!

They then invited Dana to come try it out one day.

- Dana experimented with the swing.
- Dana whirled on the merry-go-round.
- Dana had fun with the digger.
- She even made a layup.
- She had fun in the sandbox.
- She and Daniel played tic-tac-toe.
- Dana had never been happier than she was at that moment.

Dana has visited the playground every day since then, either with her father, mother, grandfather, or grandmother. Since then, many more children have visited the playground, each one unique and special in their own way. Each of them has a unique set of

113

needs, and each of them finds a unique way to enjoy playing on the playground.

Is it Possible for a Deaf Girl to Sing?

"One day," Ariel declared, "I will be a famous singer." It was Ariel's sixth birthday, and many guests had gathered at her home to celebrate. Ariel had been thinking about it all night, and now she climbed to the highest chair and exclaimed, "I will be a famous singer when I grow up!"

The entire room fell silent. Everyone came to a halt and stared at Ariel. "But Ariel, dearest, I don't see how you could become a singer," her mother said. I'm so sorry, love, but you're but you are hard of hearing.

"You're still very young Ariel, and you don't understand everything just yet," her aunt Bella said. When you're older, you will." "I'm sorry, but you're not going to be a singer," her father said.

"When you grow up," her grandmother advised, "you should go to university." "How would you make a living as a singer?" Aunt Stella asked. Is there even such a thing as a profession?" "It's completely unrealistic," Uncle Jacob said. Ben, her older brother, laughed and said, "You're talking nonsense!" "You can't hear the music, so you can't do it," her parent's friend stated emphatically. "It's just a dream," said another relative. "Why don't you become an accountant?" her mother's friend suggested. "Perhaps you should consider modelling instead?" suggested her best friend.

Ariel's face crumpled as she listened to what everyone had to say, and her eyes welled up with tears. Ariel adored her grandfather and would accompany him on trips to the zoo and the beach. They would sometimes have lengthy discussions about life and music. He stood up and said, "Ariel, you will be whatever you want to be!" You will be taught by a specialist. You'll learn which vibration corresponds to which sound this way. You will practise until you remember which vibration corresponds to which musical notes. You will be able to study the lyrics to any song you want to sing and practise them over and over again. Until you can sing so beautifully that anyone who hears you will be taken aback! You will have to work hard, and it will be difficult at first. But if you really want to do it, don't give up because it's difficult. "In the end, you'll be a singer!"

Ariel jumped out of her chair, joyfully hugging her grandfather, and replied, "I will be!" I'll be there!"

Spot is enraged!

Hi! I'm a Calming Spot! When an Angry Spot appears, I'm here to help you calm it down!

What Exactly Is an Angry Spot?

An angry spot is also known as anger instead of beautiful. Anger is just one of the many emotions we can feel on a daily basis. Sadness and anxiety are also emotions!

We all have these feelings inside of us. However, we feel the best when we are in our peaceful location. It's fine to have small emotional spots, but when they become too large, you don't feel very good. So, I'm here to show you how to reduce the size of your big angry spots to a very peaceful little size! Just like me! When you are frustrated, afraid, or hurt, your angry spot may appear. It is easier to manage strong emotions when you are calm. I know a special trick for making your angry spot calm down!

Do you want to see it? Allow me to examine your hand! Imagine four red spots on your fingers and one green spot on your tongue. Now, count the spots from one to four with me. Tap, tap, tap, and tap again. Fill your lungs with peaceful air and lavish love and care on your spots. You now know what to do. Let's take a look at some scenarios in which your angry spots appear. This looks very familiar! Remember the last time you tried something new and it didn't turn out the way you wanted it to?

This can be extremely frustrating! Have you noticed how big the Angry spot has grown?

Ahh! So, instead of yelling, you should try this trick instead?

When you start counting, you are revealing your angry spot. It's now time to calm down and shrink! Fill your lungs with peaceful air and love and care for your spots. Take a look at how the calm air really cools down an angry spot! I'm feeling so much better now!

Everyone has a unique artistic style, and I shouldn't compare myself to others.

I'm still learning, so it doesn't have to be flawless. I'm so relieved to be at peace again. Oh my goodness!

Here's another case where an angry spot becomes too big! I understand that when someone steals your toy, you may fear that you will never see it again. That's my plaything! Return it to me! Calm your English pat-down instead of stamping your feet or growling. When you are calm, you will notice that she is not trying to be mean, but rather to play. Count the number of spots from 1 to 4. Tap, tap, tap and then tap some more.

Count the number of spots from one to four. It's effective! His size is already in the Angry spot! Now fill your lungs with peaceful air and fill your spots with love. It is easier to deal with any situation when you are not present. What made you steal my dinosaur?

I thought we were playing dinosaur chase! Let's take a look at another situation where an angry spot appears. As in when you are upset because you believe you have misplaced your favourite toy. What happened to my dinosaur? It's now in the toy box! When you try to make a masterpiece but something spills, your angry spot makes it harder to find.

Sometimes your Angry Spot makes it difficult to see what a wonderful thing you have created! When your angry spot has calmed down, you'll notice that you created some amazing splatter art! When you're calm, it's easier to see the bright side of any situation. Remember, YOU have the ability to CALM your Angry Spot and turn it into a peaceful location! Count the number of spots from one to four. Tap, tap, tap, and tap again. Fill your lungs with peaceful air and lavish love and care on your spots.

You can make your own spots out of construction paper or cut them out and tape them to your fingers.

Jimmy, the jittery jitterbug

Jimmy is a Jitterbug, and he is the sweetest, kindest, and most loving little Jitterbug you could ever meet. Jimmy, on the other hand, is often shy and anxious, and he jitters. When it's Jimmy's turn to read at school, he gets nervous.

He is concerned that his classmates will mock him if he misspells a word, or that he will read too quickly, too slowly, too softly, or too loudly.

Miss Hoot, his teacher, reassured him, "Jimmy, everything is fine." "There is no need to rush, and there is nothing to be concerned about." We're all having a great time listening to you read."

That made Jimmy feel better, and he finished his reading without jittering as much. But it wasn't just reading aloud in class that made Jimmy nervous. If Jimmy was invited to a sleepover at a friend's house, he would be nervous. Jimmy enjoys his friends, but he gets anxious when he is away from home for an extended period of time.

"Perhaps I shouldn't go, Mom." When I'm gone, who will water the plants and take out the trash? What if I'm not having a good time? What? What if something bad happens to me? "Who will look after you if I'm not there?" Jimmy wondered, his voice trembling.

"Now, Jimmy," he softly replied to his mother, "I can certainly take care of the plants and trash, and both you and I will be just fine." You adore your pals, and they adore you. I am confident that you will have more fun than you know what to do with in no time!"

That calmed Jimmy down, and he happily packed his belongings for the sleepover without jittering. Jimmy's concerns did not end there. Jimmy would also tremble before going to bed.

"It's very dark. Nothing is visible to me. "What if there are monsters out there waiting for me?" Jimmy trembled. "You know, Jimmy, I used to be afraid of the dark as well," his father admitted quietly, "but there's nothing to worry about."

"I have an idea," his father said, smiling. "Let's go through the room together!"

With that, Jimmy and his father searched the closets, behind the curtains, and under the bed, but there was no sign of a monster.

"Did you find anything, Jimmy?" his father inquired, knowing full well the answer. "No, Papa," Jimmy replied as he climbed into his bed. "Well, then, the coast is clear," Jimmy's father said, tickling him as he tucked him in. "Don't worry, I'll put this little night light next to your bed so it's not quite so dark." With that, he kissed Jimmy goodnight.

Jimmy felt better as a result, and he didn't jitter as much.

119

CONCLUSION

I recommend establishing a consistent time and place for undisturbed meditation as a daily practise. This is your personal time, and the time set aside for meditation should be prioritised by you and respected by those around you.

In my experience, the easier I make it for myself to meditate in the morning, the more likely I am to practise. This is accomplished by keeping my meditation cushion set up and ready to use at all times. When I wake up in the morning, I go straight to my meditation cushion and begin to meditate. Throughout the day, if I'm feeling stressed, overstimulated, or emotional, I simply sit on the cushion for a few minutes to calm down.

Because everyone is unique, our meditation practises will be as well. Examine what you've written in your Meditation Notebook to see if anything stands out in terms of the best times of day to practise and the type of practise you prefer.

Consider your experiences over the last 10 days, then start outlining your new practise plan in your Meditation Notebook by answering the following questions:

- Was there a particular time of day that worked best for you?
- What was your favourite type of meditation?
- Do you have a favourite meditation position?
- Did any of your meditations elicit strong emotions?
- Was there a particular meditation that was particularly relaxing?

Consistency is essential. Missing a day or two can quickly turn into missing months. Continue to cultivate the habit! Even if you miss your morning (or evening or lunchtime) meditation time, schedule a quick 10-minute meditation session later in the day. A flexible practise is a long-term practise. I recommend striking your own unique balance of consistency and flexibility. You'll want to keep your practise as consistent as possible (daily, or even twice a day!), but don't make yourself so rigid that if something comes up, you miss it completely.

Open yourself up to different types of meditation. For instance, if you miss a morning meditation, you could devote your lunch break to mindful eating. Also, be adaptable in terms of the length of your sit. If you're a morning meditator and you oversleep one day, three minutes of counting your breaths might be all you have. That's fine for that morning, and it's far preferable to skipping practise entirely.

Take your three minutes, appreciate them, and see if you can schedule another session later in the day.